UNCHARTED
WATERS

UNCHARTED
WATERS

ROMANCE, ADVENTURE, AND ADVOCACY

ON THE GREAT LAKES

Mary McKSchmidt

Uncharted Waters: Romance, Adventure, and Advocacy on the Great Lakes

For information about this title or to order other books and/or electronic media, contact the publisher:

 14 KARAT BOOKS
P.O. Box 214
Macatawa, MI 49434
https://www.14KARATBOOKS.com

Library of Congress Control Number: 2018902885

ISBNs:
Paperback 978-1-7321009-0-9
eBook 978-1-7321009-1-6

Printed in the United States of America

Cover and Interior design: 1106 Design
Cover Photograph: Mary McKSchmidt
Nautical charts courtesy of National Oceanic and Atmospheric Administration

To Rubin

TABLE OF CONTENTS

Table of Contents

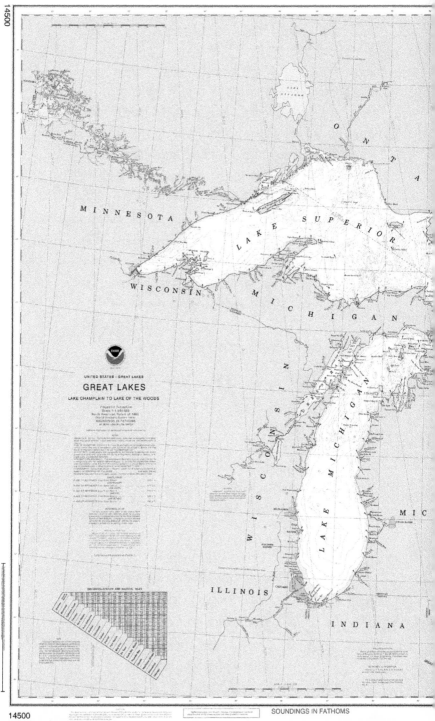

UNITED STATES - GREAT LAKES

GREAT LAKES

LAKE CHAMPLAIN TO LAKE OF THE WOODS

SOUNDINGS IN FATHOMS

14500

26th Ed., Oct. 2015 Last Correction: 11/28/2017, Cleared through:
LNM 0318 (1/16/2018), NM 0418 (1/27/2018), CHS 1211 (12/29/2017)

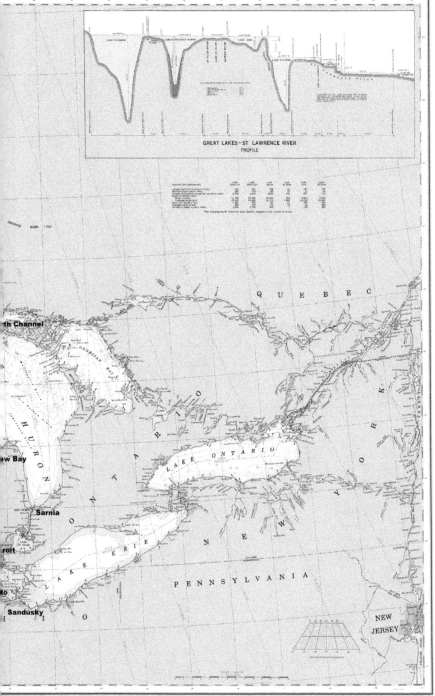

GREAT LAKES—ST LAWRENCE RIVER
PROFILE

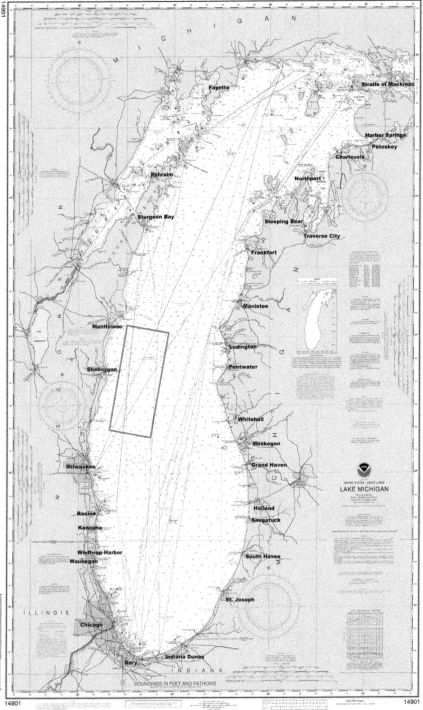

14901

14901

LAKE MICHIGAN

PROLOGUE

*M*y fingers shook with excitement as I dialed my parents' number. Standing in a cramped phone booth outside Casco, Maine, a few miles from the camp where I was teaching whitewater canoeing, I was calling less to get their permission than approval. Especially my dad's.

"My friends, Andy and Lynne—here at the camp—are traveling to South Africa for six months. They've invited me to join them. Andy's parents live in Johannesburg. They've offered to let us stay with them. His parents have even found me a potential job as a writer for *SA Tennis Magazine*!"

My words were rolling across the phone lines fast and furiously. "We're to leave in late August. I mean, when else will I have this kind of opportunity? To really explore another country? To have friends with me, a place to stay, a job? What do you think?"

Twenty-two years old, I was midway through a college degree, an education I was financing first through a full-time job at the city newspaper, then pickup jobs, and then as a whitewater canoeing instructor. My dad, a professor at Michigan State University, also loved the adventure and learning associated with travel. When I was a child, and it was my turn, I accompanied him to the university's auditorium on Saturday nights to watch and listen to travelogues. Flashing across a gigantic screen were photographs of faraway places, not merely explained but romanticized by the wandering adventurer behind the podium. When Dad's job took him to places like Massachusetts, New Hampshire, or Washington, D.C., he would pile us into the family station wagon so we, too, could see the country.

His silence that evening hung like a shroud around me. I had never crossed him and had not anticipated anything but enthusiastic support. As I waited for his reply, I grew more nervous. For the first time, I realized the enormity of my decision, and I, too, said nothing.

After several minutes, he answered slowly. "I think it's a bad idea. But you're an adult, old enough to make your own decisions, old enough to live with the consequences."

Permission. Not approval.

I never asked my dad why he didn't approve. Never really thought about it until he passed away, decades later. Now, as I reflect on his response, I think it was more than a father's concern for the safety of his daughter. Deeply embedded in him was the belief that education must come first, must be the highest priority for his children, his students, for everyone. Without an education, doors do not open. Options are limited. He wanted our future to be brighter than his distant past. He did not want us scarred by the pain of poverty. He wanted me to stay the course, to finish the degree.

One month after that phone call, I was standing, head bowed respectfully, before a uniformed South African Customs Agent glaring at me from behind the counter. I did not notice if there were drinking fountains in the Johannesburg airport. It was not important to me at the time. I did see the "Whites Only" signs above the restrooms, and they unnerved me. I was raised by a father who not only initiated and helped facilitate the first visit to campus by Martin Luther King, Jr., but also was responsible for opening doors so a black family could own a home for the first time in our community. Intellectually, I knew the Republic of South Africa was governed under a policy of apartheid. Still, the signs rattled me.

Beads of sweat dampened my armpits. Straight from camp, I had my possessions stuffed in a backpack strapped to my shoulders. My hair fell in long, stringy waves, partially hiding the top of my faded blue-denim overalls. Eyes lowered, all I saw was the Customs Agent's gun strapped to his belt, and yet I felt him undressing me with his eyes. A flaming red blush crept up my neck, burning my cheeks.

"Let's see your money," he growled, pointing to the counter.

Required by the government to purchase a round-trip ticket when I obtained the visa, I was also told I had to show enough funds to support my six-month stay in the country. Otherwise, the embassy official explained when I called to begin the approval process, the agent had the right to put me on the next plane home.

I didn't know for sure how much was "enough," but I suspected it was more than the ten $20 traveler's checks with my name on them. Long before credit and debit cards and ATM machines defined a traveler's financial options, traveler's checks were the international currency of choice. Knowing I had to find a job to finance my stay, I purchased the smallest denomination available to pad my minuscule wad of money.

Scanning the crowd were armed guards, dressed in khaki shorts and crisp short-sleeved shirts. There was not a friendly face among them. Dutifully, I pulled out the black plastic sleeve containing my checks, my heart beating rapidly as I tried to appear nonchalant. No one else had been asked to do this. In hindsight, I probably looked like an American "hippie," rather than the kind of visitor this conservative blend of Dutch Afrikaans and British government welcomed with open arms.

Glancing over at the crowd on the other side of the Customs gate, I saw alarm written all over Lynne's face. Waltzing through ahead of me, she was standing with Andy and an elderly couple, who must have been his parents. Shortly before landing, Lynne had suggested I add several of her $500 traveler's checks, "just in case." At first, I refused, insisting, "They never look." I was determined to do this alone, to bear the consequences of my decision, just as my dad had directed. But at the last minute, I tucked her checks from the same bank, in the same color, but with blatantly different names, into the sleeve.

I scarcely breathed as I watched the Customs Agent thumb through the traveler's checks.

"Okay." He finally waved me on, his irritation obvious.

I didn't know at the time that the country's policies would affect my ability to find work. When the job at the magazine did not materialize, my options were limited. Careers for women were primarily in the fields of nursing, teaching, and secretarial support.

I was untrained in the first two and told I was overqualified for the third. Worse, when I applied for the type of short-term jobs I assumed I could pick up easily—waitressing, retail sales, yard work, painting houses, even babysitting—I was told such jobs were for people of color, "certainly not fitting work for a white woman."

For the first time, a quiet fear would shadow my days as I experienced life with little to no money with which to make choices.

Several months later, I remember baking under the scorching rays of the South African sun and staring at the black wrought-iron fence enclosing a plush two-story motel. My feet glued to the rocky soil on the other side of the street, I was thinking of my three new friends from Australia and New Zealand: Jon, Anne, and Kent. We'd met at the bistro at the Carlton Hotel in Johannesburg, an American-owned hotel, where I had eventually found a job as a bar waitress. After working with them for a few months, they invited me to join them on an excursion exploring Botswana, Rhodesia (now Zimbabwe), Swaziland, and the eastern coast of South Africa. Traveling in a crotchety old white van, we made it to the coastal city of Durban, South Africa, before our funds, like the van, gave out. Our job searches were not going well. My friends were at market, bartering for food with the few remaining coins in our possession.

"You can't go with us," Kent said emphatically. "Hearing your American accent, they'll jack the prices up."

My job was to obtain fresh drinking water. My job, always, was finding the water.

Taking a deep breath, I crossed the road, empty plastic jug in hand. My heart was beating so hard inside my T-shirt, so fast, I feared someone would hear as I slowly opened the gate, stepped into the gardens, and walked toward the door. I tiptoed past the busy receptionist and down the nearest hallway. Seeing a door marked "Women," I scurried inside and quickly filled the container with water. Hastily retracing my steps, I entered the sweet-smelling gardens and felt relief pour from every muscle in my body.

"I didn't see you at breakfast this morning." An elderly woman appeared from the shadows of the building.

"Oh," I exclaimed, startled by the unexpected voice. "I'm not much of a breakfast eater."

"But this is Sunday," she continued, friendly but probing. "They don't serve lunch here and only a small supper in the evening."

"I know." My cheeks were flushing. "I'm not a big eater. But thank you."

"I'll look forward to seeing you this evening," she said with a smile.

Fighting an urge to sprint across the road, I turned and attempted a casual stroll around the side of the motel, as if the door to my room was just around the corner.

Was it wrong to take the water? Swirling in guilt, I trudged along the dusty road to our campsite. My conscience accused me of stealing, of violating values ingrained since childhood. But was it fair that water was a luxury, easily available to those with money? Doesn't everyone need water? Have a right to water? Didn't I have a responsibility to survive?

I felt sweat dripping from my hairline, rolling down the back of my neck. I was weary, hungry, and frustrated by my inability to find a job in an environment where white women were not supposed to work. Above all, I was thirsty. As I felt the stifling heat of the afternoon sun drain the energy from my body, I longed for a drink of ice-cold water.

As nightfall approached, I had no choice but to return to the only motel within walking distance. We were out of water. Again. This time, I was trembling. *Please God, don't let anyone notice me*, I prayed silently as my hand grasped the gate's latch. My tennis shoes, powdered with road dust, heels worn, edges tattered, were a stark contrast to the manicured gardens. I slipped into the motel and back out, unobserved. But as I turned to leave, I saw a silhouette shaped by the fading sun on the building's peach-colored walls.

I gasped. I could see myself handcuffed and pushed into a filthy vehicle, driven to a sweltering jail. Without money for a lawyer, there would be few options. I would be detained in a windowless prison cell for months. Best case, they'd put me on a plane and send me home, with shame as my life's companion.

Paralyzed, unable to breathe, I waited for the uniformed men to emerge.

"Here," the woman said gently, stepping toward me and taking hold of my sweaty hand. "Here, take this. I am a mother. I know what you're going through." Into my wet, sticky palm, the gray-haired woman from earlier that day placed a handful of Rands, the South African equivalent to dollars.

I felt my insides crumbling in the face of her kindness. I wanted so much to be strong, to be independent, to appear in control. But at that moment, I was none of these things.

Wrapping my arms around her briefly, I tucked my head on her shoulder to hide the tears trickling down my cheeks. "Thank you," I whispered before slipping through the gate, a jug of water in one hand, the Rands clutched in the other. I remember that, of the two treasures grasped firmly in my hands that evening, it was the container of clear liquid to quench parched lips that felt most like gold.

And gold is not something to squander.

RELATIONSHIPS: 1978–2003

One can sail any compass heading save that which points directly into the wind. Therefore, when face-to-face in a blustering blow or even the breath of a breeze, to sail forward one must first "fall off" the wind, honoring its direction.

The same is true with relationships.

THE ICEBREAKER

I remember when I first fell in love with Lake Michigan. Standing no taller than the kitchen counter, I received a gift from my mother. Actually, it was a bribe. Trying to persuade me to quit sucking my thumb, she gave me the book *A Child's Garden of Verses* by Robert Louis Stevenson.

During our mandatory rest period after lunch, I lived within Stevenson's poems. On its lime-green cover, a little boy and girl relax on the edge of a pond, framed by flowers and leaves of every color and shape imaginable. On the pond, a tiny boat sails effortlessly. A robin, perched on a floating leaf, serenades the little girl with a pink ribbon in her short, blond hair.

The illustrations created my fantasies; the memorized verses became the fabric of my dreams. When my mother encouraged us children to post lists for Santa on the refrigerator, I knew exactly what I wanted.

"A cabin in the woods near a lake," I asked her to write at the top of my list, for I longed to be an artist, a writer, and live immersed in the book's romantic illustrations of nature.

My siblings gave me a hard time. "Santa can't give you something like that," they told me. But I kept it on my list, year after year.

The summer of my eighth year, my father piled the three eldest of his six children into the family station wagon to go camping at Orchard Beach State Park outside Manistee, Michigan. Scrambling from the car to a fence marking the edge of the world, I looked down a steep bluff at miles of clear, blue water, shimmering in the sunlight. I was mesmerized.

For an entire week in August, we dove like fish into the waves. Burrowing deep into the sand, we created moats around our castles, rivers meandering through our kingdoms. After supper, we raced each other to the split-rail fence, guarding the sandy cliff, high above Lake Michigan. Perched on posts, feet dangling over the edge, we watched in awe as the sky became a brilliant array of pinks, reds, and oranges. We waited, spellbound, for the night sky to come alive with the twinkling of thousands of tiny stars, and for Dad to point out the planets.

My greatest fear was that I might never see the lake again.

I amended my Christmas list that winter. I wrote, "I'd like a cabin in the woods near Lake Michigan." It remained at the top of my list until I went to college and was no longer eligible for the refrigerator postings. And while initially my college curriculum was filled with the lyrical words of poets and authors, and my backpack stuffed with notebooks, pens, paintbrushes, and canvas, everything changed after the six-month trip to Africa.

"I will never be poor again!" I told my mother when I returned. The woman—who had once listened to a child's dreams of being a writer, who had encouraged me as I studied grammar, punctuation, and sentence diagramming, who had given me a book so I could learn to type and allowed me to practice on her manual black-and-white Smith-Corona, who had been my biggest cheerleader when my part-time job as a high school reporter for the local newspaper evolved into full-time employment as one of the first five women sports editors in the country—said nothing as I switched my major from English to business. Words were replaced with numbers, palettes of paint with spreadsheets, essays and poems with income statements and balance sheets.

Only much later would she admit I'd returned from Africa a different person. Hardened. Intense. Focused. For fear, once it has planted its seed, burrows dark, winding tunnels through the heart. Even dreams risk being lost forever.

And then, three years later, a business degree and job in hand, I met the boy on the lime-green cover.

▲ ▲ ▲

Introducing myself to Rubin is Sharon's idea. My first administrative assistant, she is worried about my social survivability in Saginaw, Michigan, an industrial city renowned for bowling and beer. I, a 1977 graduate of Michigan State University, who lettered one year in tennis, am interested in neither. Sharon, who quietly is coaching me through the political intricacies of my first corporate office job, is convinced the guy on the second floor is perfect for me. She insists he is polite, fun loving, and good-looking—and he plays racquetball, as do I.

I don't believe one should mix one's personal and professional lives. At least that's what I tell Sharon. In truth, I am very uneasy about approaching a man socially. In the late 1970s, it just isn't done. At least not by me. But a few months later, when I see him standing near the drinking fountain, I muster up my courage and walk toward him.

"Hi," I say boldly, although my flushed face reveals my thin veneer of confidence. "My name is Mary. I was just transferred here. I'm an assistant buyer on the third floor, and I hear you play racquetball."

He waits, saying nothing. Feeling no way to retreat gracefully, I plunge forward.

"Well, I was wondering if you'd like to play sometime."

His blue eyes peer at me from beneath thick, blond eyebrows, raised in surprise. For a second, the corners of his mouth hint at a smile. His entire demeanor, from his broad shoulders to his straight, confident stance, seems to silently whisper a reply. "Oh, really!"

Mortified, I shrug and start walking away. "Unless you're afraid to be beaten by a girl," I add. That does it.

We play racquetball two days later. He annihilates me. Rubin, twenty-one points. Mary, zero.

As a result, I don't challenge him to a rematch. Instead, I suggest canoeing down the Au Sable River, sliding through February's icy waters lined with crusted snow banks and frozen patches of land. Canoeing is my sport, one that combines my appetite for adventure with my romantic view of nature. And while I'd never paddled in the winter, the thought of immersing myself in the glistening white snow and the crisp, fresh air fills me with excitement.

But I watch in horror as his feet break through the ice and into the frigid waters of the slow-moving river while he's pulling the stuck canoe through an ice jam. Soaked from his thighs to his feet, his jeans immediately begin hardening with ice. We are still two hours from our designated pullout. When his only comment is a puzzled "…and this is fun?" I have a hunch Sharon might be right about Rubin.

From the beginning, ours has been a relationship of playful challenges and spirited negotiations between two competitive but very different personalities. If paddling a canoe through the icy bite of winter was my test for Rubin—and it was—his invitation to crew on a Hobie Cat on the second weekend of May is his chance to scrutinize me.

Rubin shares an apartment with Larry, his best friend and sailing buddy. They sail in A Fleet, a group of boats commanded by topnotch catamaran sailors. Trophies lining the shelves in their apartment tell me they are accustomed to winning regattas.

"Larry has to work this weekend," Rubin says early that week. "Would you like to crew for me?"

"I'd love to!" I respond instantly. Only later do doubts begin blanketing that self-assured exterior. My summer sport is whitewater canoeing, not sailing. I have never been on a Hobie Cat, a sailboat consisting of two pontoons connected by a trampoline and boasting a colorful set of sails. I was a guest once on a friend's thirty-eight-foot sailboat but slid off the edge of it while trying to attach the line to the post when we docked. I hugged the pole, wood splinters and all, to keep from falling unceremoniously into the water. The experience was not a great credential for sailing, much less racing.

My first challenge is figuring out what to wear. I have no idea save one: I want to look thin. Spinning my body in front of a mirror for a couple hours Friday night, I analyze every possible clothing combination until settling on a turquoise bikini to match my eyes, a pair of cutoff jeans that come just two inches below the bikini to show off my legs, and a T-shirt.

When Rubin picks me up the following morning, a thin box with an orange ribbon around it is sitting on the passenger seat. The ribbon is the same bright tangerine color as the stripe on his sail. Inside the box I find a set of new sailing gloves, women's size medium.

I am determined to live up to his expectations.

Exhilaration soars through me the first time I feel the catamaran lift above the water. I am clipped to a cable attached to the mast in something called a "butt bucket," a colorful nylon contraption that looks like an adult diaper. As the boat edges toward the sky, I lean back in the bucket as far as I can, legs fully extended with feet curled over the lip of the pontoon. Gazing at the clouds overhead, I feel as if I am flying!

A shimmering spray of water rolls off the other partially submerged pontoon, exploding into a bubbling white wake off the stern. The boat hums as it races across the lake, propelled by an increasingly powerful wind. A gust lifts us still further, and I am standing, one with the boat, perpendicular to the water. I steal a glance at Rubin, standing beside me as we teeter between euphoria and an icy dousing into the lake below.

"Release the jib sheet." I hear his voice over my shoulder and immediately pull up on the line clutched firmly in both hands, unsnapping it from the teeth of the jam cleat. Sailing terminology is foreign to me, but this term, "jib sheet," Rubin says I cannot forget. This thick braid of line attached to the headsail is my primary responsibility as crew.

Immediately the wind escapes the sail and the boat flattens, drenching me as a wave splashes over the bow. Out of the corner of my eye, I see his right hand on the tiller, the left adjusting the line controlling the shape of the mainsail.

"Okay. Pull it in slightly." I draw down on the jib sheet, clamping it back in the metal fitting, and watch the air quickly fill the sail. Instinctively, I look back and notice one of our closest competitors has capsized. The giant sails float eerily in the water, and the undersides of both pontoons are exposed. I see two bodies swimming furiously toward the overturned catamaran.

For a second, a shiver of fear flashes through my body. *Not us!* I tell myself, tightening my grip on the jib sheet.

"Watch the water." The stern tone of Rubin's voice pulls me back. The intensity written on his normally easygoing face is sobering. "When you see a dark patch in front of us, that's a gust. Let the sail out, or we'll flip, too."

Beads of water dribble down my forehead, blinding me. I shake my head furiously, trying to rid myself of the icy mixture of rain and lake water rolling down my face. My teeth are chattering from cold as I stare alternately at the water and the little red ribbons on the jib. My job, Rubin had explained earlier in the morning as we sailed to the start line, is to adjust the jib sheets until the ribbons, or "telltales," point straight back. That's how we maximize boat speed. And winning regattas is a combination of good starts, smart tacks, and boat speed.

The T-shirt clings to my shivering body as early spring cloaks me in a misty rain. The regatta, the first of the season, is held at Clark Lake outside Jackson, Michigan. Only when we registered our boat with the race committee that morning did I learn the regatta is called "The Icebreaker Regatta." And while at the time I had second thoughts about my attire, now I would give anything for something warm to shield me from the bone-chilling cold.

"Can you see the mark?" Rubin's voice redirects my focus. Squinting, I stare at a horizon, blurred by the veneer of rain, the similar grayness of water and skies.

"No," I admit ruefully.

"Look to one o'clock," he continues, pointing ten degrees off the bow. "See it? It's just a tiny spot of red. We can't make it yet. Tell me when it's at three o'clock. That's when we should be able to tack over and round the mark."

I still see nothing. The trickle of water rolling into my eyes doesn't help. Nor does my body, shaking uncontrollably from May's frosty weather. Nor the lack of my prescription glasses, left behind—deemed too unflattering for a date. Most likely, the truth lies in some combination of all. And while eventually I would learn to spot the mark immediately, even before Rubin, that would not be today.

As we near the finish line, an imaginary line between the committee boat and a buoy, I hear men hollering at their crews, most of them women. Their voices bark orders, their tones demeaning. I cringe. *There's no way I will stand for that type of treatment, race or no race,* I think.

Rubin's voice, I notice, is strong, loud enough to be heard, but respectful. He speaks as a patient instructor teaching an eager student. And while he sees no reason to think or talk about the past, I will eventually learn that he has studied to be a minister, taught fifth-grade math, and coached seventh- and eighth-grade girls' volleyball before he joined the corporate world to design and create store displays for Wickes Lumber, one of the largest lumber companies in the country. A calming presence notes his demeanor, even in the throes of competition.

Despite the weather, despite the chills running through my body, I listen carefully, intent on learning, determined to be the perfect crew. When we are first to cross the finish line, he leans over and plants a warm, soft kiss on my frozen cheek.

"Would you like to borrow rain gear?" a woman from a nearby boat hollers above the wind as we head to shore for lunch. "I have a spare coat in the car." I slide my arms into the jacket, grateful for her kindness and thrilled to feel cloth next to my skin.

Not once do I glance in a mirror.

Two weeks later, when I open the apartment door, ready to join Rubin on my next regatta adventure, he places a pair of slick, bright yellow overalls and a matching raincoat in my arms. Perhaps he believes a good captain always cares for his crew, particularly when the crew has helped him win the top trophy in her first time on a Hobie Cat. Perhaps he doesn't want me catching pneumonia in the inevitable stormy weather accompanying regatta weekends. But perhaps—just perhaps—he likes that turquoise bathing suit nearby on sunny days.

I'll never know. When I ask him now, almost four decades later, he just smiles.

OPENING THE DOOR

"*D*on't you dare touch that door."

I stop abruptly, dumbfounded, and look at him.

"Opening the door is my job," he insists, his smile softening the unfamiliar tone in his voice.

"But I can do it."

"Not when I'm with you." I think about it for a moment. In my late twenties, I am already committed to what will become a lifelong interest: pioneering paths for women in worlds dominated by men. And there's no question, I like to be in control. But opening a door?

"Okay."

Now he chastises me every time I forget and automatically reach for a knob or handle. It's a reminder. I'm not alone. I don't have to do everything.

This sunny but cool December afternoon, I remember and pause in front of two large oak doors trimmed in granite. I feel his hand on my elbow and watch as he opens one of the doors to the Alumni Chapel on the Michigan State University campus. Tucked romantically alongside the Red Cedar River, the chapel is an easy walk from the business center, the place I have spent most of my time the last twelve months.

"School is not something I enjoy," I had explained to Rubin earlier, when I first considered returning to get my Master of Business Administration degree. "But I've got to be able to go toe-to-toe with the financial minds and negotiate effectively for monies I want in my budget. I've got to understand accounting—be stronger with numbers."

The voice was that of my parents: etched into my fiber by a dad with a Master's degree in accounting and a PhD in economics from the University of Oklahoma and a mother, a graduate of Incarnate Word College in Texas—a published writer, and the public information director for one of the largest, most successful public school districts in Michigan. In our family, there was never any doubt: learning was key to a person's success. But the path we selected was our own.

"With interest rates in the high teens, I don't want my career tied to a lumber company, connected so closely with the ups and downs of the housing industry." My analytical left brain dominated my thinking—had, since returning from Africa. "Going back to school to get an MBA lets me start over to find a company in a recession-proof industry."

It is Rubin's idea to visit the chapel. We have been walking the grounds of a campus I knew first as a child accompanying my dad to his office, then as an undergraduate, and most recently as a student of the MBA program. We are celebrating my graduation and the job offer from a hospital supply company, to be a surgical sales representative in Milwaukee, Wisconsin. I had a choice: Portland,

Oregon, a harbor city on the Pacific Ocean, or Milwaukee, a city perched on the western shores of Lake Michigan. And while the wandering adventurer was drawn to the unfamiliar ocean coastline, something tugged at me, as I stood on a rocky cliff in northern Milwaukee, overlooking the sparkling waters of Lake Michigan.

The quaint-looking chapel is interdenominational. I have never been inside it, but looking up at the gentle, smiling face of my best friend, a man I'd been dating exclusively for the last three years, I can't think of a better place to stop and say a prayer of thanksgiving, or anyone I would rather accompany me.

The door to the chapel opens, and we are immediately flooded with light streaming from the long, narrow stained-glass windows, towering over the altar and lining the cream-colored walls of the room. Bits of color dance across railings, podiums, and pews, constructed simply but beautifully from oak. Despite the darkness of the beams supporting the ceiling, there is a natural brightness to the space, an energy that is warm and inviting. I feel as if I am in hallowed space, a room created by artists, designed to feel the presence of God.

We walk slowly, hand in hand, to the front pew. And it is here in this sacred space that Rubin asks me to marry him. And while I never considered marriage part of my future, for once in my life I do not stop to think. I allow my heart to have its say.

TWO BY TEN

"We can make that first mark if we start on a port tack." With just five minutes to the start of the race, I hear the familiar but dreaded words. Rubin has stalled the catamaran in the middle of the starting line, that imaginary line drawn between the committee boat and a giant orange buoy. Pointing the boat directly into the wind, he eyes a tiny piece of yarn tied to the side stay, one of the wires used to support the mast. The sliver of yarn and the bow of the boat point to a spot just to the right of the first mark. If we cross the starting line on a port tack, a tack that means we have no rights and must yield to all boats sailing from the opposite direction, we have a straight shot at making the mark.

Because tacks require skill and precision timing, the intent of the race committee is to design a course that forces racers to make multiple tacks, zigzagging into the wind before rounding that first mark. Since the mark must be rounded on its starboard side, the race committee positions the orange buoy defining the starting line so that a starboard tack is favored. That ensures each boat must make at least two tacks on the first leg of the race. But every once in a while, the wind shifts at the last minute. Those with nerves of steel will sail an apparent collision course into a fleet of hard-core racers screaming toward the starting line on starboard tacks.

That would be Rubin. And his crew. Me.

"One minute," I holler as I see the blue flag, off the stern of the race-committee boat, drop from sight. "Fifty-nine, fifty-eight, fifty-seven . . ."

Twenty-nine other catamarans are bunching up behind the powerboat, vying for the top spot. They jockey for clean air and the position closest to the wind, hugging the committee boat until the exact second the red flag is raised, the gun is fired, and the race begins.

We are on the other end of the starting line. Alone.

"Thirty, twenty-nine, twenty-eight . . ." My voice is loud and controlled, even as my heart races and adrenaline surges through every muscle of my body. The jib sheet is clutched in one hand; the other hand is raised so I can see my watch.

"Starboard." Already the first boat, straddling the invisible starting line, hails us with a forceful warning. Sailboats with the wind filling their sails from the right side of the boat, the starboard side, have all rights in racing.

"Hold your course," Rubin responds, jerking the tiller so we duck behind the pontoons of the other boat. "Let it out!" he shouts, and I quickly dump the air from the jib to avoid hitting the next boat. "Sheet it in." I pull on the sheet to fill the sail, to gain momentum, and to keep us moving along the starting line.

"Starboard!"

"Starboard!"

"Hold your course!"

"Starboard!" Voices are screaming at us, like seagulls attacking a fishing trawler. I alternately yank and release the jib sheet to avoid slamming into an oncoming boat. I no longer notice the fleet, concentrating only on the closest boat, the one we are seconds from hitting.

"Ten, nine, eight, seven . . ." My voice continues as we weave in and out through the fleet. Our pontoon misses the rudder of another by inches.

"Starboard! Starboard!"

"Harden up! Harden up!" Rubin shouts, and I pull the sail tight to the wind. "Hold your course," he yells to the other boat.

"Three, two, one," I continue. At that moment, I hear the gun explode from the stern of the committee boat and see the red flag raised. Sheets are pulled in, sails tighten, and pontoons begin lifting above the water.

"All clear," the voice behind the megaphone shouts after us.

Alone on a port tack, we are in clean air, screaming across the water toward the orange marker, barely visible on the horizon. Other boats flop over to separate from the pack, to find fresh air, to pursue the boat with the commanding lead. Us.

Finishing first across the finish line, we head to the beach for a break between races. My fingers claw at the neoprene wetsuit glued to my body, fingers so numb I can barely grasp the zipper. Drenched from the spray of the catamaran's hulls cutting through the frigid waters of Lake Michigan, my hair drips icy beads down my neck.

On the western side of the lake, the Wisconsin side, I am always chilled by the time we haul the catamaran out of Lake

Michigan—even after living here six years. Rubin says this is because the predominantly southwest winds blow the warmer surface water across the lake, depositing it on the Michigan side. That makes sense. It can also be that my body adjusted better to cold when I was eight years old. But this struggle to stay warm, the constant battling of wind and waves, is eroding the loving connection I once felt for this lake.

Above the din of wildly flapping sails and the roar of crashing waves, I hear the shouts of other racers as the fleet of catamarans streaks toward shore. Hobie Cats, Nacras, and Prindles skim across the water before slamming into the wet sand and screeching to a halt. Clad in the cumbersome butt buckets, wetsuits, and life jackets, bodies hastily dismount and pull the heavy pontoons through the soft sand and up to higher ground. They drag the bows into the wind to keep the northeasterly wind from shredding the sails. To the oiled and scantily clad sunbathers lounging on towels nearby, bedlam has overtaken the leisurely Saturday afternoon at the beach.

"Nice start," Dennis's English accent rises above the other voices. He and Sue are top competitors, accomplished racers of catamarans and iceboats. I see Rubin helping to turn their boat into the wind, chatting with them and the other racers on the beach. I should be helping, too. Teeth chattering, eyes watering, and with two fists the size of snowballs pawing at the zipper of an unflattering, skintight wetsuit, I think of only one thing.

Can I make it in time?

And then miraculously, Rubin is standing in front of me, unzipping the black suit and freeing me to race to the women's bathroom of the Racine Yacht Club.

Steam mists the giant mirrors as a group of shivering women huddle around sinks. We stand in silence, splashing hot water over numb, red fingers.

"Do you believe it's July?" a muffled voice eventually rises above the lowered heads.

"No."

"Did you jump in the water between races?" asks another.

"Are you kidding?"

"Men are so lucky."

Words slowly tumble from thawing lips.

"I quit drinking liquids around seven o'clock the evening before a race," I confess.

"Men and their 'two-by-ten' ritual," laughs another, referring to the tradition of gulping two beers by ten o'clock on race mornings.

"I could make a fortune if I could figure out a way to eliminate bodily fluids from women."

"Any ideas?"

"Not yet."

Slowly they begin filing out of the bathroom, heading for the bar to grab a sandwich and maybe a small sip of water. The race committee hopes to start two, maybe three more races if the wind holds. No liquids for me until nightfall.

I linger, relishing the returning feeling to my fingertips, and stare at the body in the mirror. Shoulder-length pigtails continue to drip cold water down my body. Soaked, my hair accentuates my square jaw, the long lines of my father's broad shoulders. A T-shirt, wet from the droplets of condensation inside the wetsuit, clings to my thirty-five-year-old body. I can see the effects of gravity as my body ages, and I realize it is becoming increasingly difficult to look good in a wetsuit.

"I am tired of being wet and cold in the middle of July," I admit to the face in the mirror. Sometimes, like today, the chill is caused by the wind propelling the cat at speeds so great a wall of spray douses the one closest to the bow. Me. Often the teeth-chattering cold penetrates because racers are on the water for hours without a break. A decision is made to hold continuous races. Or worse, the wind dies. Regardless, I have dangled from the lip of the pontoon many a time, relieving my bladder into icy waters.

"It is time for a boat with a head," I declare before leaving the warmth of the restroom.

But what do I do? We have been racing catamarans together for nine years. Rubin loves the thrill of competing, of pitting his skill and knowledge against other top-tier racers. He's known for his port starts, his commanding knowledge of racing strategy, his understanding of the rules. Our consistent top-place showings have earned him a reputation across Michigan, Illinois, and Wisconsin. And while he crews for friends on monohulls, it's not the same as being the captain of your own boat. What do I do?

Little did I know the sly dog was waiting patiently for the purchase of a bigger boat to be my idea.

THE INEVITABLE

"Just call me a boataholic," Rubin told me shortly after we began dating. We were visiting his family's pale-green cottage, tucked in a clump of maple, spruce, and oak trees on the shores of Sanford Lake, northwest of Saginaw, Michigan. I remember him shoveling the drift of snow away from the front door, building a fire in the fireplace to warm the gathering room, roasting hot dogs on long, snowy sticks over the flames, and pouring Lancer's Rubio wine in plastic glasses to toast our first Valentine's Day together.

"This cottage is only thirty miles from home, so we lived here on weekends, summers, every vacation," Rubin reminisced. He talked about tooling around the lake in an aluminum fishing boat with a five-horsepower motor before he was seven years old, waterskiing by the time he was eight, repairing boat motors by eleven, and sailing his neighbor's Aqua Cat catamaran by twelve. He bought his first boat, a twelve-foot Sea Devil sailboat, when he was fifteen and his first Hobie Cat shortly after turning twenty-one. There was never any question. Boats would always, at least partially, define this man's life. But this?

I stand, mouth open, staring at a thirty-foot Sea Ray Sedan Bridge powerboat, dry-docked for the winter.

"You're kidding!" I exclaim. "It seems so big!"

I suppose that was my doing. I had prefaced his search for a boat with the caveat, "We know lots of guys who buy a boat, and then two years later suffer from 'two-foot-itis.' Let's get a boat big enough that we're not constantly trading up and losing money in the process." But this? The jump from an eighteen-foot catamaran to a thirty-foot yacht leaves me feeling hopelessly inadequate.

The salesman wisely stands aside, saying nothing. He's leaving the selling to Rubin.

"Come on up," Rubin says excitedly as he climbs the ladder leaning against the hull. "Believe me, you can't have a big-enough boat on Lake Michigan."

I can almost feel the adrenaline surging through his body, hear his heart racing with the thought of possibly owning this lakefront condominium. For that is how he views larger boats, "affordable waterfront property."

"Come on, I'll give you the tour!" He tugs at my arm as he ascends the stairs to the fly bridge. "You can see for miles up here and drive the boat from either here or below, depending on weather. Here, sit behind the wheel."

"But a powerboat?" I ask, sliding behind an unfamiliar, foreboding instrument panel. He has been researching boats for months, crawling in and out of companionways, talking with boaters and salespeople. I know his first choice was a new, thirty-four-foot Catalina sailboat, but the price was way outside our range. This boat, while used, is in immaculate condition and affordable.

"Any boat is a great boat," he says with a disarming grin. "And a powerboat has a lot more room below. The way I look at it, this can be our summer cabin."

That makes sense to me. The stern of the boat is a perfect back porch. Two steps down is a cozy, plush living area with a galley in which to make meals and serve cocktails. There is a berth with a queen-size bed and, most importantly, a head boasting not only a toilet but also a sink and a shower. A warm, dry boat with a head!

After several more visits, we sign the papers. And then we drive to the Racine Yacht Club to celebrate.

"So, Rubin," I say, after toasting our purchase. "How much will it cost to take the boat out to the reef light and back?"

"Well, let's see. The light is three miles off shore, so six total miles, not including what it takes to get to the harbor entrance. At three-fourths of a gallon per mile, one dollar and forty cents per gallon . . . it will take a little over eleven dollars and twenty cents—I'd say figure about twelve dollars total—to get from the slip to the light and back."

And then it hits me like a giant wave, spilling over my body and tumbling me across the scraping sand. I relive the months, standing penniless on a roadside in Africa, subsequent years laboring in often crummy jobs to pay for a college education, the relief at scrounging together a down payment for our first house, and the joy at finally having a small sum of money in our savings account.

The ice is diluting the rum and Coke® of my celebratory drink as I watch the golden light of autumn skip across Lake Michigan. The salesman had explained in detail the fuel efficiency of this model of Sea Ray. "It uses only three-fourths of a gallon per mile," he'd explained, his fatherly smile wide and endearing.

Elbows propped on the bar at the yacht club, my feet dangling from a stool, I clasp my hands together with my thumbnails pressed tightly against my lips. It's not that we hadn't been weighing the decision carefully, deliberating for days. But words create pictures in my mind, not numbers. Only now, after listening to Rubin calculate the cost of powering our thirty-foot powerboat the three miles out to the reef lighthouse and back, does it become clear.

"I can't do it," I whisper in a voice choking with the horror, the fear, the knowledge that I have made a terrible mistake, one that will ruin our lives. And it is my fault, for in the delegation of responsibilities, it is my job to manage our finances. And while we can afford the boat, slip fees, and winter storage, fuel will decimate our savings. Every penny we earn will be poured into the lake. Literally.

The celebratory drink sits on the counter in front of me, barely touched. Through the giant, wall-size window behind a colorful assortment of liquor bottles standing on the shelf behind the bar, I see the Racine Reef Lighthouse boldly breaking the thin line dividing water and sky.

"Mary, look at me," Rubin says softly after several moments of silence. "We don't have to buy this boat. We can go back and tell the salesman we made a mistake. But, remember, we don't actually have to leave the slip. It's a cottage. That's all. Just a cottage."

I would like to think there was a voice inside me recalling the serenity of a sailboat slicing the smooth waters created by a westerly breeze off the Wisconsin shore, the exuberance of harnessing the wind and waves to surf atop this mighty lake, the oneness with the universe when stretched out in the silence of a sailboat while staring at summer's puffy white clouds floating across a powder-blue sky. But I do not yet have that kind of relationship with sailing or the lake. At this point in my life, it is all about the money.

Leaving our unfinished drinks on the bar, we return to the salesman, arriving shortly before closing time. Years later, I still recall with fondness his kind smile, his wrinkly eyes, and his large hands ripping up the contract.

That next spring, 1988, we purchase a new thirty-foot sailboat, trimmed in the soft gray of evening's first shadows. And because Rubin's selection for a boat name—that string of letters painted on the stern that provides a thumbprint to one's identity—is *Boat*, I take control and name our floating cottage, *The Inevitable*.

NO ROPES ON A BOAT

itting cross-legged in the bow of *The Inevitable*, I feel ridiculous. A red, black, and white bandana is tied across my eyes, blinding me to the inquisitive stares of those walking along the dock and past the sailboat. Most pause and ask what I'm doing, for in my hands I have a rope . . . no . . . line . . . no . . . sheet.

My answer draws applause.

I am learning to tie a knot called a "bowline" in less than ten seconds. Blindfolded. It is Rubin's idea; he insists a bowline is critical to life on a sailboat. In an emergency, he says, I must be able to tie it quickly, even at night. Looping the end of the "jib sheet" over the "bow pulpit," I think about sailing lingo. In my hands I finger what looked like a rope when he first placed it in my hands, what felt like a rope, but now that it has touched a pier, is anything but a rope.

"There are no ropes on a boat," Rubin explains patiently. "They are called 'lines.'" There are dock lines, which secure the boat to the slip; anchor lines, which, if the anchor holds, keep the boat safely nestled in a cove or bay. However, once the line is confined to the boat, it usually morphs into something else.

For example, *halyards* hoist. The *main halyard* hoists the mainsail to the top of the mast, the *jib halyard* raises the jib or headsail, the sail set forward of the mast. There is a *spinnaker halyard*, which on our boat is the *spare halyard*, my least favorite. Legs dangling from an unflattering bosun's chair attached to the spare halyard, my pockets stuffed with pliers, screwdrivers, and an assortment of other tools, I slowly am cranked up the mast to make repairs. The job has nothing to do with being mechanically minded. I just weigh less than Rubin.

Sheets control speed by moving the sail in or out. Two sheets are tied with bowlines to the jib. Crank the *jib sheet* in when going to weather, that point of sail close to the direction from which the wind is coming. The sail flattens, causing the boat to heel and pick up speed. Let them out, and the sail spills air, slowing the boat. The adjustments are different when the wind is off the side or beam of the boat—or off the stern. But the concept is the same. The sheets control the movement of the sail, and the sail determines speed. A *mainsheet* controls the mainsail. Tied to the boom, rather than the sail, it, too, is used to maximize speed. A *traveler line* shuttles the boom from one side of the boat to the other, perfecting the trim of the mainsail.

Initially, knowing these rules was good enough. A catamaran racer for our first nine years together, my job was to use the sheets to control the jib. My body stuffed in a butt bucket and extended over the water, I would stare at little red ribbons on the jib called "telltales." By adjusting the jib sheet grasped in my hand until the telltales pointed straight back, I helped win regattas.

After we transitioned to a monohull, five new lines were added to my sailing vernacular. All affect the trim of the mainsail. The *boom vang* lowers the boom; the *topping lift* lifts the boom. The *cunningham* fastens to an eyelet on the front of the main and is used to eliminate the wrinkles or "luff" of the sail. The *leech cord* eliminates the flutter on the back of the sail. An *outhaul*, stretched alongside the boom, controls the tension at the foot of the sail.

I never touch these lines. Perfect sail trim is Rubin's job.

The line I hold in greatest esteem is the *reefing line*, the one we frantically grab to reduce the mainsail when unexpected gale winds knock the boat on its side. And while I can tie a bowline blindfolded in seconds, I have yet to master reefing the main single-handedly. But I'm working on it. It's not just that I thrive on challenges. Knots and lines are one thing. Accurately flinging a rescue buoy in heavy air is another.

Best to learn how to keep the boat flat.

THE HELMSWOMAN

I eye the transient slip looming before me, with one hand gripping the wheel of our sailboat and the other resting nervously on the engine's throttle. My eyes dart from the wind indicator on top of the mast to the approaching pilings framing the entrance to the narrow slip. The bow slices through the water, and I watch for any sideway slippage that might indicate a wayward current.

I don't notice the heads in nearby boats turning to watch, the raised eyebrows, the tanned faces registering surprise to see a five-foot-five woman with short blond hair as she stands on tiptoes behind the giant wheel of a sailboat, docking in heavy air.

A gust slams against the mast, and the boat shudders, trembling in the wake of nature's unexpected fury. A second blast off the side, and the boat heels slightly, veering off course toward the stern of a yacht docked in the adjacent slip.

Tension cuts through me, and I see Rubin spin around to look at me from the bow of our boat. Too slow and the wind will control this dock landing, I remind myself. I increase the pressure on the throttle, and the engine roars, challenging the sound of the wind whistling through the rigging. The bow turns, heading toward the open slip. I cut back the throttle, slam the engine into reverse, and gun it to keep the bow from crashing into the dock.

For a brief moment, the boat stops abruptly in the middle of the slip, and Rubin throws lines to the waiting, outstretched arms of the Charlevoix harbormaster. "Nice docking, Skipper," he hollers as he grabs the lines, quickly wrapping them around cleats before the next gust roars through the marina.

"I'm just the helmswoman," I yell above the wind. "The guy with the scruffy beard is the skipper." I am under no illusions. The person calling the shots on our boat is not I. There is only one reason, one embarrassing reason, I am at the helm.

I can't throw.

As one who attended school before the passage of Title IX of the Education Amendment, the 1972 legislation prohibiting discrimination against women in any federally funded education program or activity, including physical education, I never learned to toss anything.

I see myself wildly flinging dock lines toward willing hands, whacking someone in the face, or missing their outstretched hands completely. Without lines looped around posts or tethered to cleats, I see the boat surging forward, hear the fiberglass splintering as the bow hits the dock, discern the accusatory whispers of "throws like a girl" floating across the marina, and feel the red flush of humiliation creeping up my cheeks. The realistic possibility of disaster creates a recurring nightmare so horrible that I am afraid to leave the dock for fear of returning.

Initially, Rubin tries to guide my arm through the proper throwing motions, but the terror of being labeled "a sissy" creates a whirlwind of nerves inside me and slams shut any chance of learning. Very quickly he changes tactics, suggesting I master life behind the wheel. He insists I am too small to fend off, to keep the boat from hitting the dock should he have difficulty maneuvering it into the slip.

"We're a team," he explains, "and a team finds ways to work together."

I don't want to disappoint. But my confidence is as fleeting as perfect air on a perfect day. And so several days later, as I stand behind the wheel at the fuel dock at Northport Marina off Traverse Bay, tension tightens every muscle in my body.

"The best way is to back in."

"I know," I mumble.

"Spin around in the channel so you can motor past the spot. Once you're past and begin backing, remember you need enough speed so you—not the wind—control the boat."

"Okay."

"You should have plenty of room. Just get the stern in, and the guys will grab the lines."

"Okay." I eye the empty space on the wall. At tops, it's fifty feet, ten feet on either end of our boat. There is absolutely no margin for error. On one end of the spot is a Danforth anchor, its dagger-like claws dangling from the bow pulpit of a sailboat. On the other end is a Grand Banks trawler, a favorite of Rubin's. When I asked him why, he said he likes the sleek lines of the boat. I certainly don't want to ding up those lines.

"The wind is going to want to push you into the other boats, so speed is critical."

"I know." My voice does not reflect confidence as I survey the last spot on the wall. There are no vacant slips for the night. It's the wall or another several hours of sailing into the late evening.

"Do you want me to do it?"

"No, I can do it." I am reluctant to give up the wheel, to admit defeat without an attempt. It goes against some internal code of honor, some streak of craziness running through me. I try to visualize parallel parking the boat. A car is difficult enough. But a boat? *Think positive thoughts,* I remind myself. I see myself, with one hand on the wheel, the other on the throttle. I know I can do this. I know I can. But I silently whisper a quick prayer to my guardian angel as a precaution.

"Okay, then let's go," Rubin says, and the dock master tosses him the lines tethering our boat to the fuel dock.

I inch the boat into the channel, my heart beating so fast it feels as if my chest might explode. Instinctively, I glance at the arrow on the top of the mast, reconfirming the direction of the wind and trying to gauge its strength. So much of docking is by feel.

Just past the fuel dock, I spin the boat so the bow can lead us slowly past the open space. Rubin says nothing. We have learned over the years that his voice is the only voice I hear when engrossed in docking. One word from him, and my concentration breaks; I look up, assuming an imminent catastrophe, and throw my delicate balance between motion and mental focus into disarray. The result can be disastrous.

Backing is even harder than docking.

When reversing the boat, the stern leads. It is easy to get discombobulated. I used to turn my head back and forth constantly, panicking when I saw the bow going in the opposite direction from my steering. Of course, it would have to. But I'd forget, get confused, and panic. Most of the time I'd holler for Rubin to take over. He'd drop the lines and race back to the wheel, and I'd shakily try to toss lines to waiting hands or scramble off the boat to cleat us off, my confidence shattered.

It was ugly.

And then I noticed a boat handler in the San Juan Islands who was backing boats while standing on the other side of the wheel, his back to the bow. He steered the stern. The rest of the boat followed. No distractions.

I adopted the "San Juan" method of backing.

We are several boat lengths past the open space on the wall before I flip the engine into neutral and then reverse. I quickly move to the "San Juan" side of the wheel to steer the stern, increasing the pressure on the throttle. For a moment, nothing happens, and I quit breathing. And then the boat begins gliding through the water.

I glance back once to make sure I have enough speed so that I, not the wind or current, am controlling the boat. I adjust the throttle slightly. Totally absorbed in the movement of the boat, I wouldn't notice if a firecracker were to go off next to me.

Once I have the momentum, I back down the speed and slowly guide the stern into the open space. Like parking a car, I begin straightening out the boat. Docking lines are tossed, caught, cleated.

We are secure.

Someone starts clapping, and others quickly join in. Only then do I see the small crowd assembled on the pier and feel the edges of a blush, creeping up my face. Only then do I take a breath and smile.

But the one with the widest smile is the guy standing in the bow.

UNDER THE STARS

"It's magical here," I say, after we secure our anchor in the weedy bottom of Snail Shell Harbor of Michigan's Upper Peninsula.

It is the deep, royal blue of the water that I notice first; it forms a mirror on which the limestone bluffs at the harbor entrance reflect the golden hue of the descending sun. The birds are flitting about the shore, chattering as they dart about leafy trees and search for the perfect branch on which to spend the night. The skeletons of stone buildings on the land stand empty, remnants of a once-bustling community. It was here in Fayette in the 1800s that iron ore was smelted into pig iron and shipped to steel foundries in the southern cities of the Great Lakes. Now, it is a ghost town, the backdrop for a state park. As evening slides into night, the people disappear, and a peaceful silence envelops the harbor.

"It's so romantic," I murmur. "I think anchoring is going to be one of my favorite things about sailing: the feel of the boat gently tugging against the anchor line, the quiet rocking of the boat like that of a cradle, the oneness with the sky, the wind, the water . . ."

I stop, thinking back to the two summers I spent guiding young girls in canoes down whitewater rapids in Maine and leading them on trails threading through the mountain ranges of New England. On the overnight trips, we would stretch tarps over lines tied between trees to protect us from rain. But if there was no threat of rain, we often pulled our sleeping bags out far enough to fall asleep under the sky. I remember huddling in a mummy bag, only my nose and eyes exposed to the crisp Maine air, while I stared at the stars. I was sure my future lay in being a rugged outdoorswoman.

But that was before Africa, before financial security became my primary focus, before I silenced the longings of my right brain and acquiesced to the demands of my left. I have not hiked a trail or slept under the stars since my return.

Suddenly I realize Rubin has been silent since dropping anchor. "What?" I ask, puzzled. "What's the matter?"

Streaks of pink, as soft as a baby's blanket, slice the graying evening skies.

"This is a fairly safe anchorage, provided the wind doesn't shift," he replies in a voice that chills my enthusiasm. "If it switches to the northwest, if it comes through that small entrance into the harbor, we may be in trouble."

"Why?"

"We dropped anchor with the wind out of the southwest, fully protected by land. If the wind comes through that channel and blows hard from the northwest, there's a good chance the anchors won't hold. Our boat and all the others anchored here could pull loose from this rocky, weedy bottom; they could potentially crash against the pilings of that old pier."

"Oh."

"But you're such a light sleeper, maybe you'll wake up if there's a wind shift."

"Oh."

▲ ▲ ▲

Have I slept? I'm not sure. What I do know is I am suddenly wide awake. I lie there, the darkness of the cabin rendering my eyes useless, as if in a cave far below the earth's surface. While I cannot see him, I hear Rubin's steady breathing as he sleeps soundly at my side and feel the boat rocking as it has all night. But something is different. Something has changed. What?

I stare into the darkness and listen intently, waiting to hear the noise that may have stirred me from a fitful sleep. But night seems to have smothered all sounds save the distant clanking of the halyards of other sailboats nestled in the small harbor.

There. There it is, a rhythmic slapping against the side of the hull. Waves. WAVES! Waves mean wind!

Immediately, I bolt up and swing my legs off the edge of the V-berth, while grabbing a wall for balance. Dressed only in a flimsy cotton nightshirt, I scramble up the steps and into the cockpit.

The wind whips my hair about my face into a frenzy of tangled knots, as I emerge from the companionway. The stars—romantic companions earlier—have disappeared. Lights flickering on shore break the blackness; only a few anchor lights glow softly from the top of masts scattered throughout the harbor. Straining my eyes, I can just make out the ominous shadows of hundreds of rotten pilings, spears piercing the waters near shore, remnants of the old shipping pier. Despite the darkness, the sign nailed above the new long pier, framing the southwest shore, is as visible as a highway billboard:

FERRY DOCK
ABSOLUTELY NO BOAT DOCKING!
VIOLATORS WILL BE PROSECUTED.[1]

I feel the wind on the back of my shoulders, like two powerful hands pushing me toward the stern. The boat, rocking side to side, suddenly lurches as it pulls against the anchor line, and I'm thrown against the wheel. My fingers wrap around the grab bar for balance, and I turn to face the storm. Despite the bullets of rain beginning to pepper my face, I can see the whitecaps edging the giant swells rolling in from the open water. The bow, as good an indicator as any weather vane, points northwest, directly toward the harbor entrance.

"Rubin, wake up! Wake up! There's a wind shift!" I shout, sprinting back down the companionway to find a pair of jeans and don shoes and a raincoat. In minutes, we are both on deck.

Already, the halyards are clanking wildly against the masts as the wind whips the harbor into a frenzy of large, white-topped haystacks. I hear the frantic shouts of other boaters as they, too, rush to cockpits to gauge the severity of the storm, to determine how best to stay safe.

"We're dragging anchor!" Rubin yells, clutching the lifeline as he races to the foredeck. Squinting to see the shore through the stinging rain, I see we are much closer to the pilings, closer to another boat whose owners have yet to surface from their cabin below deck.

I start the motor and holler at the other boat, hoping to awaken its occupants. They, too, are dragging anchor, inching closer and closer to the deadly grip of the old pier. But it is as if my voice is a whisper in the howling fury of the storm.

I hear Rubin's voice in the bow.

"What?" I shout.

"Put it in forward!"

I can barely see his outline huddled underneath the bow pulpit as he pulls up the anchor line. How do I maneuver the boat when it is so dark? And how do we reset the anchor? How do we keep from dragging again? From smashing into other boats? Worse, how do we keep from drifting into that pier? Keep the jagged spears from puncturing our hull and sinking our boat? What do I do?

"Neutral."

I slide the engine into neutral, while struggling to hear his voice above the din of the storm—the one blowing in off the lake and the one raging inside my head.

"Neutral . . . Forward . . . Reverse . . . Neutral . . ." The noise of the halyards, the wind violently shaking the rigging, and the rain pounding the deck heighten the sense of dread seeping through me like the first chill of a dense fog.

"We're free," he yells.

Free? To do what? What am I supposed to do?

"Head for the ferry dock," he shouts.

"We can't do that!"

The sign is clear. No boat docking.

Rubin is rushing toward the stern. "We have no choice. It isn't safe out here." He grabs the wheel. "Get fenders out on the port side. I'm going to try to swing us around so we're pointing into the wind when we dock. Get lines ready. Be prepared to jump off the boat as soon as it's close to the dock. And get the lines around the closest pilings fast—as fast as you can."

"Rubin, it's the ferry dock. What if the ferry comes in the morning? Then what? It says 'Absolutely No Docking.' We can't dock there."

Raised to respect authority, I never question orders; I adhere to the law, no matter what. In protesting, I would like to say I do not fully understand the risks; I am still too new to sailing, too naïve. But, in truth, old patterns die hard. I am more terrified of docking under a "No Boat Docking" sign than facing the merciless clutches of a raging storm at midnight.

Rubin pulls our boat alongside the ferry dock. And so do all the other boaters. All save one, the one I tried to hail earlier. I can just barely see the outline of the white hull, pinned against the ragged edges of the old pier. Faintly, above the wind and clanging of boats, I can hear the revving of its motor, make out the fragments of shouting voices.

"There's no way that motor is strong enough to pull them off that pier," says one of the people standing on the ferry dock with us, eyeing the distant boat.

"Maybe, if we took a dinghy and put a line on his bow, we could pull him off," says another.

"It will need to be a long line to get any traction."

"And if that doesn't work, we need a line long enough to bring back to one of our winches, and we can try to crank him off."

Immediately, people are jumping back on boats, grabbing anchor lines, and knotting them together. The man with the dinghy starts his motor, and Rubin and two other men quickly disappear into the night. The rest of us stand like a flock of ducks huddled safely together under the stark white "Absolutely No Boat Docking" sign as the storm pummels the fresh, new boards of the ferry dock. Only when the sailboat is finally pulled off the pier and safely rafted off a boat tied to the dock, do we all climb down into our companionways for the remaining few hours of night.

Shortly before dawn, accompanied by the fresh, sweet smell of the night's rain wafting off land and before any possible confrontation with the captain of the ferry, we sail in search of a new port. I have no doubt it will be a harbor with a dock to which we can tie a spider web of lines to keep us safe and secure.

But there is a side of me that wishes we would anchor another night in Fayette. I suspect it is the same side that used to curl up in a sleeping bag alongside a river, listening to the roar of the rapids downstream while waiting for the stars to appear. It is a side I have almost forgotten.

LANDLOCKED

"I would rather be boating," Rubin mutters as sweat drips down the side of his face. He stands in the middle of the fairway, a five iron in his hand. Waiting. Watching the foursome in front of us. Waiting. In the distance, someone holds the pin while another hunches over a putter. Waiting. The man with the putter pauses. Backs away from the ball and then takes a couple of steps. Squats down to analyze the putt. Returns to the ball. Takes a couple practice putts. Steps back again.

A man in the foursome in front of us rolls his head back, drops his club, and throws his hands in the air in exasperation but says nothing as he stands under the blazing sun, waiting. Rubin shakes his head, sighing deeply. The back of his freshly starched short-sleeved golf shirt is soaked with perspiration. The only life flourishing in the stifling heat and humidity of this July afternoon in Nashville appears to be the cicadas. Their high-pitched rattling buzz provides a steady din, occasionally escalating to a crescendo of intense commotion. I am listening to them now, as I wait, thinking about golf.

The sport is part of my job—has been since 1990, when I accepted a position where my role is to be in relationship with hospital executives throughout the United States. It is a career path that first transferred me to Columbus, Ohio, to oversee our corporate business in the Midwest region, and now in 1994 to Nashville, Tennessee, to manage relationships with the for-profit healthcare chains.

▲ ▲ ▲

I remember my first management retreat roughly ten years ago, the site for it tucked in the forested beauty of Lake Geneva, Wisconsin.

"Are you sure you don't want to go shopping?" the national sales manager asked for the fifth time.

There were two of us at the time, two women among the twenty-one field managers responsible for sales in the United States. My cohort decided not to golf. I, however, was determined to be one of the guys, to be accepted, to be a member of the team.

Standing on the red tee box of the first hole, I struggled to calm my nerves and settle my stomach. I was a beginning golfer, learning a sport I knew was part of the fabric of business relationships. Behind me was silence. My peers stood, a circle of men around the white tees, watching, waiting.

Why did Ed put me in the first foursome? Why couldn't I have been in the last?

We were playing scramble, a game where all four members of a team hit their own golf balls. The best shot is the point from which the next round of hits occurs. One of my teammates had driven his ball in the middle of the fairway. We had a shot. All I needed to do was be respectable—not to whiff or send the ball in some errant direction.

Taking a deep breath, I began my backswing.

"Wait!" a voice hollered. "Stop!"

I froze, the shaft of the driver suspended in midair.

"You have the wrong ball!" Ed yelled, racing toward me from the crowd of spectators. Reaching down, he picked up my ball, replacing it with a bright-pink golf ball, the color of ribbons I wore in my hair as a child.

A roar of laughter echoed behind me, off the trees, and down the fairway. Flabbergasted, I turned and saw guys doubled over, several rolling on the ground in hysterics.

Slowly, I raised my club and then crushed that pink ball, sending it soaring down the middle of the fairway, past my teammate's white ball so that it became the point from which our team would take its next shot.

From that day forward, I became a long-ball hitter. My putting was erratic, often pathetic, but I almost always hit a long drive off the tee box. However, golf, like any sport, takes practice. And weekend afternoons were time for practice.

▲　▲　▲

"You know I have to play golf," I say, trying to wipe the sweat off my forehead with the clammy back of my right hand. Actually, I revel in the sport that places me outdoors for hours and allows me to stand on tee boxes overlooking some of the most spectacular settings in the world.

Rubin says nothing.

Managing simultaneous careers has been tough, particularly with my transfers from Illinois to Ohio and then, Ohio to Tennessee. Rubin has built a strong reputation in his field and recently started his own business as a manufacturer's representative for point-of-sale merchandising in Nashville. What is missing in his life—in our lives—is boating. My commitment to career and the excessive travel required, in addition to transfers further and further away from the Great Lakes, ultimately necessitate the sale of *The Inevitable*. And while we charter sailboats in the Caribbean, the San Juan Islands, and Traverse City, Michigan, it is not the same as leaving all roughage of life in the parking lot each weekend and sailing out to greet a fresh, blue horizon. In the cockpit of a sailboat, there is an intimacy between us, an unspoken language that draws us together.

Golf is not the same.

To my surprise, living in Tennessee has also rekindled a quiet anxiousness about water. Spoiled by life in the Great Lakes region, we didn't think to inquire about water prior to moving to a suburb south of Nashville. Only later, when summer water bills reached highs of $300 a month, did we learn our community did not have access to its own water supply. Every drop is purchased and piped from Nashville. No more leaving the faucet open while brushing teeth. No more obsessing about the perfect lawn. Conserving water quickly became a way of life.

"I'll tell you what," I continue. The siren song of the cicadas pierces the air, and I feel as if my head will burst from the commotion and intense heat and humidity as we stand, waiting. "Let's make this interesting. From now on, let's bet a buck a side and a buck overall based on handicaps. The money must change hands at the end of the round. What do you think?"

"Okay," he says, turning to look at me, his eyes twinkling and the hint of a grin redefining the expression on his face. "You have a deal." He extends his hand to shake mine. "Do you have your dollars for today?"

Of course, I don't and have to take out a three-dollar loan at the end of the round. But the money is collected immediately when we arrive home and placed in a designated pocket of his golf bag for winnings. I am informed future loans will carry interest charges.

From that day at that green on that hole, I never again receive a "gimme putt" from my husband. My handicap drops to a respectable fifteen strokes. His, however, falls from eighteen strokes to ten, and his designated pocket bulges with bills.

Our golfing friends say I got snookered.

I think it depends on the game.

IN SEARCH OF BALANCE

I am lying in bed two years after moving to Tennessee, and the bright red numbers on the clock beside my bed read 1:15 in the morning. I can hear the deep voice of a man talking in the apartment next door, women laughing, the clinking of glasses, several voices competing simultaneously for the limelight, a hearty laugh, and then a loud shush. Someone remembers that others live in close proximity—others who might be trying to sleep, who might have an alarm clock set to buzz at 5:15 AM, who might be facing a tough day at work, and who are decades past the resilient energy of youth. One of those others is a woman in her late forties. Me.

What was I thinking?

True, the job is a giant step up the corporate ladder of success. I have responsibility for overseeing a $140 million business, a chance to build my own team, to find answers in a complex, challenging, and highly competitive healthcare environment outside the walls of the nation's hospitals—i.e., home care, surgery centers, long-term care pharmacies. It is an honor to be considered for the position, seductive to be offered the job. Both have "me" written all over them.

At least one side of me. The other side—the side drawn out by the man who makes me laugh, who sands down the intense edges of my personality, who knows me and loves me just as I am—is back in Nashville. With Rubin.

I am alone in a northern suburb of Chicago.

And so, I send emails to co-workers at 9:00 at night before I leave the office and at 4:30 in the morning when I can't sleep. I listen to voice mail before I go to bed and the minute I awaken. Issues and challenges swirl constantly in the backdrop of my mind. The job consumes me; soon it defines me.

"I know it isn't healthy," I tell Rubin on the phone in the evening. "And it's not good for my staff. I'm pushing them too hard. It's just that my mind churns nonstop with work. It has become my entire life."

But what can I do? The question gnaws at me while I jog through streets touched by light's first breath. A daily ritual that began decades ago to keep from gaining weight, jogging has become sacrosanct, as critical to my life as breathing. In days defined by hospitals, hotels, airports, offices, and conference rooms, jogging connects me to the outdoors. It allows me to explore the richly diverse worlds to which I travel on business, provides alone time to ponder the never-ending questions accompanying me through life. I find, as the sun transforms the gray canvas of dawn to the bright, fresh-smelling colors of day, jogging is a time when prayer flows easily, when answers often magically appear.

One morning, as the steady hum of Chicago traffic drones in the background, I know what I can do—must do—and I race to the apartment to phone Rubin.

"We have always talked about living on a boat." The words are tumbling over each other, fast, brimming with excitement. "Why don't we buy a boat for me to live on while I'm in Chicago?"

A week goes by.

"Have you found a boat yet?"

"I wasn't sure you were serious."

"I am."

Two weeks later, we are the owners of a ten-year-old, forty-foot Hunter sailboat. Hoping to influence my lopsided life, I name the boat *Balance*.

"What are you going to do in the winter?" people ask. The wind, snow, and ice force boats off the water by November.

"I'm not sure yet. Do you know anyone who hates winter?" I reply. "Who goes south? Who may be looking for someone to house-sit while they are gone?" I ask everyone.

Jogging along the wetlands bordering North Point Marina in Winthrop Harbor, I listen to the chatter of birds delighting in the day's beginning and watch the golden circle of light inching above the dark-blue horizon. As the first sparkles of morning sprint across the lake's surface, I pray for what feels like a miracle.

And then it happens. A coworker directs me to a woman in need of a house sitter in Lake Forest, Illinois. The white Cape Cod, tucked among towering trees and shade gardens, is located several blocks off Lake Michigan. The discovery allows me to keep my jogging ritual of welcoming the dawn at water's edge, of inhaling the beauty, strength, and healing power of the massive lake at my side. In April, when the ice thaws, I return to the boat.

For three years, I watch the pink spray of sunrise splash across skies edged by the midnight blue of the lake. The long walk along the pier to my car each morning—past forty other boats—allows me time to make the transition from the life of my heart to the reality of my days. The only person on the pier in business attire, I brave heavy winds, rain, sleet, and even snow to pursue the career of my choosing.

My choosing.

Driving back to the boat each evening, I feel a sense of peace settle about me the minute I see Lake Michigan through the windshield. "Hello, Lake," I say with a giant smile. With that first step on the pier, I feel as if an angel is lifting all heaviness from my shoulders, freeing me to see, smell, touch, hear, and experience all the glory of life . . . all the joy in living. Accompanied by frogs, crickets, birds, and mosquitoes, I sit in the cockpit, as the soft, black carpet of night becomes the backdrop to an ensemble of glittering lights frolicking across the skies until they near the lake's horizon. Then blackness.

Only the moon dances on Lake Michigan. And her dance begins to awaken the buried dreams of a child paging through a book of poetry.

GOOD INTENTIONS

"When I saw you come out of the companionway with a knife, I knew we were in trouble."

"I mean, we really did bond as a team. We were all scared shitless."

"But you looked so composed. It was just that knife that gave you away."

"Did you know Greg fell over the bow railing when we were docking?"

"Don't get us wrong. It was fun and everything. But can we just go out for a beer next time you want a team-building exercise?"

My intentions were honorable. I mean, hadn't I once been told to ride a zip line if I wanted to be part of the team? To fall backwards, arms folded against my chest, into the arms of peers? To wander blindfolded through woods and across streams, tethered to those with whom I worked?

Rather than our normal Wednesday afternoon staff meeting, I invited everyone for a leisurely sail on Lake Michigan. It wasn't a requirement. My administrative assistant opted out, choosing to wish us *bon voyage* from the dock. But everyone else signed up, thinking it would be great fun. And it was . . . at first.

The midday temperatures were in the high seventies, the lake relatively flat with little one-foot rollers. Predictions were for winds of ten, maybe twelve knots. My plan was to roll out the headsail and head roughly two miles out on Lake Michigan. I had never sailed the boat without Rubin, but after checking and rechecking weather forecasts, it appeared to be a perfect Lake Michigan afternoon. And with just the headsail out, what could go wrong? I was a little worried about docking, but I had nine fairly athletic adults who were willing to help out, even though they had little boating experience. And docking always made me nervous.

On the way out of the harbor, pairs of willing and excited hands loosen the roller furling line, wrap the jib sheet around the winch, grab the winch handle, and crank the billowing white sail in just far enough for a comfortable, flat sail. Some people find places in the cockpit; others dangle their feet over the rail. Someone stands in the companionway serving beer, water, and soda, and laughter echoes out over the water.

Two miles east of the harbor entrance and well within sight of land, we decide to crank in the sail, drop the swim ladder, don life jackets, and go for a swim. That is, until I notice a line of black clouds forming to the northwest and dark ribbons of wind on the water bearing down on us.

"It's probably best if we turn around and head back without the swim," I tell the crew of lounging bodies in the cockpit. Already I feel the wind filling the sail and the boat starting to heel, or roll on its side. With a crew of novice sailors, heeling is the last thing I want to do.

"I'm going to point into the wind, so we can shrink the size of the sail. It will make the ride back more comfortable. Once the sail starts flapping, Gary, you release the blue jib sheet—just free it from the winch. Brian, you take this roller furling line and begin cranking in the sail. Those of you up on the rail, keep your heads down, so you're not smacked by the lines."

Surprised faces flip around, trying to gauge the seriousness of the situation. My voice is calm, so they watch momentarily before continuing their conversations.

"All right, heading up," I say to those in the cockpit, for Rubin has taught me always to announce any change at the wheel. The freed jib sheets crack through the air, the sail luffing loudly as the wind pours past.

"It won't roll in!" Brian exclaims, pulling fiercely on the line designed to crank the headsail into a tight white shroud around the forestay.

"Here, take the wheel and keep it pointed into the wind."

I, too, try to pull in the sail. Nothing. Greg tries. And Mike. The roller furling line is stuck.

The ink-splotched clouds etched in an eerie metallic gray, the vanishing sunlight, and the sudden gusts whipping through my hair all gnaw at my confidence. I pull out my cell phone to call Rubin in Nashville, six hundred miles away. No bars. No signal.

"Brian, are you okay at the wheel?" I ask. He is the only one with any boating experience.

"Sure. I'm good."

"Let's head back to the harbor. We'll keep the sail way out so the boat stays flat."

One hand clutching the safety line, I hasten up to the bow and tug on the roller furling line, spun around the drum. It doesn't budge. My mind is racing. We've got to get the sail in before we try to dock the boat, but it's clearly stuck. What if I just drop it, like we do each winter? Just release the jib halyard and let the sail fall to the deck?

"Okay, I'm going to have Brian point us back into the wind," I announce when I return to the cockpit. "Watch out for the lines. We're going to drop the headsail. Greg, this is the release lever. When I tell you, pull it straight up. Theresa, this is the halyard. Try and keep it from getting tangled so the headsail comes straight down. As it drops, I'm going to pull the sail on deck so it doesn't spill into the lake."

White foam now tops the waves surrounding the boat, splashing wildly against the hull as Brian points "to weather"—meaning into the wind. I hear the wind whipping through the rigging, and a knot of desperate urgency builds in my chest.

Greg releases the lever on my command, and I crouch next to the mast, ready to pull the giant sail onto the foredeck, to free us from the wind's control. But the sail will not come down.

Billowing storm clouds appear to be sprinting toward us as the wind increases, and the lake froths wildly in all directions. We must get off these waters. But with this much sail, we'll crash when we dock. I don't know what else to do. The sail will not roll up or come down. What do I do?

Again, I pull my cell phone from my pocket. No service. Forcing myself to look unruffled and in control, I head back to the stern, take the wheel, and sail toward the harbor entrance. How do I navigate into the harbor, through the narrow channel to our slip, and dock the boat with a sail filled with air? *Think,* I tell myself. *Think.*

Giving the wheel back to Brian, I grab the eyelet on the headsail, hoping I might loosen the knot and rid the sail of the sheets, freeing the sail from the wind's grasp. The wind defiantly yanks the sail from my hand, leaving me no choice but to go below. Seconds later, I emerge from the cockpit, knife in hand.

I slice the sheets attached to the back of the sail.

In that second—when the sail escapes and flies freely off the side, when the boat slows momentarily, as if surprised by the change in command—I know we'll be okay. True, even an unfettered sail will fill with air as we approach the slip. But the odds feel more manageable.

For the next twenty minutes, I explain the challenges of docking the boat with a headsail flapping in heavy air. "We'll motor into the harbor and down the channel with little difficulty. But the minute I begin turning the boat into our slip, the wind will find and fill the sail, thrusting us forward. I'll slam the engine into reverse immediately. Two people will use boat hooks to grab the lines on the dock. The back line is critical. Another will jump off the boat when we are abreast of the dock, grabbing the line tossed by another."

People volunteer for the roles they feel they can manage. We discuss worst-case scenarios. We rehearse timing: who does what, when. Over and over we repeat the procedure until we enter the harbor entrance. And then there is silence, save the wind whipping the sail and the lapping of waves in a harbor darkened by the fury of what I think is a squall. Later I would learn a tornado has touched down ten miles to the north.

The dock landing is perfect, not a scratch on the boat. The lines hold us off the dock as the sail flies out over the pier. The moment the boat is secure, I pull out my cell phone and call Rubin. He talks us through how to roll the unruly sail by hand into the drum.

"You guys are great! Truly amazing," I say to my crew as we walk off the dock. "And no, I did not know Greg toppled over and was hanging off the bow pulpit. And yes—absolutely. Next time, I promise we'll just go out for a beer."

But the day reinforces what I already know. I need my captain back in my life.

Many months later, it happens. I accept a position working for the CEO of Baxter Healthcare, bridging the relationships between our executive team and that of our clients. I become a road warrior, traveling almost eighty percent of the time, with dual offices in Chicago and Nashville. The address on my driver's license is the same as Rubin's: Brentwood, Tennessee. But I live on airplanes, spend nights in hotels, days in windowless conference rooms. My respite from the pressures and demands of life remains "our cottage," the forty-foot sailboat docked in Winthrop Harbor. For the next five years, I work the perfect job for me, for us, as we continue the dance called dual careers.

But for most of the dance, I am alone.

VIEW FROM THE TOP

"How are you doing?" Rubin hollers from below. "Can you see what's wrong?"

Can I see what's wrong? One cheek is pressed against the cold mast, and I am taking deep breaths of air to steady myself. My knees and arms are squeezed so tightly around the top of the mast that my muscles scream for relief.

"Are there screws missing? Anything like that?"

Mustering up my courage, I pull my head and shoulders back to take my first look at the harbor. Fifty-six feet below me, more than fifteen hundred boats are docked at the largest marina in the Great Lakes. And while I have jogged around the perimeter many times, it is only now, from my perch above, that I see the enormity of the highly structured boating community. Long, narrow piers extend toward the wide channel in the center of the harbor: eleven piers on the south side and seven on the north. The runabouts and small sailboats occupy the slips to the west. As my gaze moves east, the waterways, channels, and boats increase in size until I see the mega-yachts, tucked along the rows just inside the breakwall.

When we first began exploring marina possibilities, that part of my brain always preparing for worst-case scenarios felt vulnerable. It's the chronic worrier in me. A deserted pier on a quiet weekday evening would make it easy to observe a lone woman strolling out to her boat. And should an intruder slink down the companionway and trap me below, there would be no back door from which to escape. I would be alone. No one would even hear my screams.

As a result, the first things I noticed when we drove out to investigate North Point Marina, a fairly new facility adjacent to the Illinois Beach State Park, were the giant locked gates at the entrance to every pier. Signs warned that security guards patrolled the marina twenty-four hours a day. A boater we met in the parking lot told the story of a sailmaker who forgot the security code and climbed over the gate to deliver a sail. He was arrested despite the legitimacy of his presence on the pier. No code, no entrance, no exceptions.

Perfect.

Floating docks were the first thing Rubin noticed. Constructed on buoyant floats, the docks stretched across the surface of the water, allowing dock and boat to move in harmony. Once lines were tied and the boat secured, the lines would not have to be adjusted as weather and water levels fluctuate. Rubin could return to Nashville each Monday morning, knowing the boat and its inhabitant would be safe.

My legs still wrapped firmly around the mast, I release the stranglehold grip of my arms and turn to see the lake. While I have always been humbled by its seemingly infinite size—infatuated with the dance between sun and wind on its surface—to see the lake from above fills me with wonder. In some mysterious way, this lake defines a part of who I am, who I hope to be.

Suddenly the chair in which I am dangling lurches forward, my legs yanked free of the mast. I swing wildly from side to side as feet and hands flail helplessly through the air. Frantically, I reach out and grab the mast and again steady myself. Looking down, I notice Rubin walking toward the bow. With each step, his weight on the deck makes the mast oscillate like the pendulum of a grandfather clock.

"Don't move!" I scream.

It takes me a few minutes to regain my composure. Finally, I glance at the oversized bosun's chair in which I have placed my life and eye the tools sticking out of the pockets: several screwdrivers, a wrench, and a pair of pliers.

I had never touched tools other than to hang pictures until I met Rubin. Together we have gutted, remodeled, and built homes and rental properties in Wisconsin, Illinois, Ohio, and now Tennessee. He has taught me to use a power drill, hammer nails, hang drywall, and even string electrical wires. The electrical lesson was in Ohio.

"How do we know if I did it right?" I asked as we jogged together in a nearby neighborhood. (He ran with me in those days before he accused me of overdosing on distance.)

"The house won't burn down."

I looked in the direction of our house, scanning the sky for smoke.

"Oh."

A siren wailed in the distance, and my heart skipped a little. It drew nearer and nearer until I saw the flash of a red fire truck roaring down the main road to our home. Picking up my pace, I darted ahead, still searching for the telltale gray clouds of a fire.

"Rubin, they're turning into our neighborhood!" I was sprinting. "They're in our driveway!"

He finally picked up his pace. It was the neighbor's fire alarm.

Despite his patient teachings, I am not mechanically minded. Leaning back in the bosun's chair, I contemplate the project in front of me. He's the genius at fixing things. I am the wrong one to be up here.

"What do you see?" he hollers from below.

"How do I know what's broken if I've never seen it in working order?"

"Is the halyard tangled?"

"No. It's on a white plastic roller that's really worn. Could that be it?" I shout back.

"I doubt it. Check the screws. Tighten everything up there."

Pliers in one hand and a wrench in the other, I shake for fear of dropping one or both on the deck below. "Don't drop these tools or they'll puncture a hole in the boat," Rubin warned me earlier. My thighs burn from the pressure of clinging to the mast. Despite the cool breeze drifting across the marina, sweat beads down the sides of my face. I have no idea what I am looking for.

"Okay. Take a mental picture of everything so you can draw it for me," he says finally, before lowering me to the deck.

It takes three grueling trips up that mast before Rubin finds a solution. By the third trip, a crowd of onlookers has gathered. In addition to tools, the cameras of four neighboring yacht owners dangle from the bosun's chair, for I have told them the view of their boats from above is magnificent.

Several weeks later, as Rubin and I motor into Winthrop Harbor from a Sunday afternoon sail, I hear my name shouted by a group of men piled in a small, motorized inflatable dinghy bearing down on us. Beers in hand, they are frantically waving, trying to get my attention.

How do they know my name? The lessons of an extensive workshop on self-defense are ingrained in me. Avoid eye contact with strangers. Keep one's demeanor mean, tough-looking. Do not answer questions. Above all, do not say "hi." As a result, I have worked hard to be invisible at this marina.

Rubin starts laughing as they near. "They're our boat neighbors."

In the bottom of the dinghy, I see a case of Kendall-Jackson Chardonnay.

"Mary, we've been waiting for you. We have a gift we want to give you before we leave. A thank-you for the amazing photos you took of our boats! You should go into photography. Your shots are incredible!"

At the time, I shrugged off their comments. But it was a hint, dropped in my lap by the universe. Perhaps, if I'd listened, it would not have taken me so long to realize a camera, not a calculator, was the perfect tool to accompany me through life. Perhaps I would have heard the voice of the artist inside me, buried for so many decades underneath a long list of to-dos.

But I was too busy to notice.

AUTUMN CROSSING

*T*he sail across Lake Michigan is beginning as the first hint of light touches the eastern sky. Buoyed by forecasts predicting sunshine, southwesterly winds of fifteen knots, and three-foot waves, we decide it is the perfect October day to make the thirteen-hour sail. We've crossed the lake a dozen times together on vacation, but this sail is different. We are sailing our boat to its new slip in Western Michigan, a mile-and-a-half from a house we someday plan to make our permanent home.

Ten hours into the trip, I brace myself, taking a deep breath when the bow plunges into a trough between waves. The boat shudders as a wall of water rolls along the deck, spilling into the cockpit. Cold rain stings my face, the droplets peppering my foul-weather gear. As the icy water swirls around my feet, I shudder.

If I can just see the lighthouse, I'll be okay, I think to myself. My eyes are glued to the horizon. Logically, I know we are too many miles from land to see the blinking light of "Big Red," the lighthouse marking the harbor entrance to Lake Macatawa. But strapped in a safety harness to the boat's pedestal to keep from being washed overboard, I am hoping for a miracle.

Rubin is at the helm, his face grim but his demeanor calm. Normally, my job is to be at the wheel as Rubin trims sails and checks charts. Instead, I am hanging over the side of the boat, my insides erupting unexpectedly as I spew the contents of my stomach into Lake Michigan. I promise myself this is the last time I cross this lake.

"Don't worry about it; everyone gets seasick at some point," Rubin yells above the howling wind.

"Have you?" For a brief second, my eyes shift from the horizon to my husband.

"Sure," he grins through the rain. "I ate two Polish sausage dogs before a night race from Bay City to Alpena and had my head over the rail, puking my guts out the entire race."

In his own way, he is trying to help.

I watch his broad shoulders battling the wheel, fighting the combined forces of wind and waves to keep us on course. We have a sliver of the headsail out to try to keep the boat sailing toward harbor. Glancing at the compass, I notice the winds are switching to the northeast, right on the nose. One can sail a boat in any direction other than directly into the wind.

"We can't make it to Holland," Rubin shouts, making no attempt to mask his growing concern. "The wind has shifted, and these waves are too big. They're pushing us south. We'll try to make Saugatuck instead. Here, take the wheel while I check the charts."

I grab the wheel.

Quit shaking, I order my body, but to no avail. My mind is drifting back to stories I've read about the *Edmund Fitzgerald* and other freighters crushed and sunk by the violence of storms racing across the Great Lakes. Rain bleeds into tears.

No lighthouse greets boaters approaching the Kalamazoo River entrance, only tiny red and green harbor lights. "Keep the red light on the right when returning to harbor," Rubin has explained long ago. "Red Right Returning." But the lights are too small to spot from afar. Instead, I scour the horizon for the 200-foot sand dunes framing both sides of the river.

I know the Kalamazoo River is narrow, shallower than the entrance to Lake Macatawa, and so the increasing size of the oncoming waves creates a new all-consuming fear. Large swells make it more difficult to control the boat in the channel, and the shallow water increases the probabilities of bouncing off the riverbed in the trough of a wave, of potentially crashing into the breakwall. I remember Rubin's words earlier in our marriage.

"The trick in a storm is to approach the channel on the sheltered side of the pier, the leeward side. Throttle up the engine and cut diagonally across the harbor mouth slightly into the waves. That keeps you in control. If you go too slow and surf into a narrow entrance during heavy seas, the waves will roll the boat into the wall."

My teeth chattering, my body shivering, I am in no shape to tackle the Kalamazoo River entrance. Reading my thoughts, Rubin takes the wheel as we near the harbor lights.

At the time, I have no idea the Saugatuck harbor is one of seventy-six recreational harbors on the Great Lakes. With limited funding available, the U.S. Army Corps of Engineers does not dredge the recreational harbors on a regular basis. Dredging depends on the availability of congressionally earmarked dollars. Our boat draws six and a half feet below the waterline. Without dredging to keep the river at least nine feet deep, we will hit bottom when river levels are low or sediment runoff high.

But on this stormy October night, we somehow make it safely into the narrow mouth and navigate upriver to an open slip at the Singapore Yacht Club.

Later, standing in the shower at the yacht club, I close my eyes and feel the steamy water slowly thawing my frozen body. The world is rolling, walls rocking as if I am still at sea. When I emerge and return to our boat, I tuck my head into Rubin's chest and wrap my arms tightly around him.

After a couple of minutes, he holds me out so he can look in my eyes.

"Well," he says, his eyes smiling, "did you think about work?"

Boating, even in the worst possible conditions, provides balance to my life. So, too, does my husband.

PURSUING DREAMS: 2004–2007

One must first learn the mechanics of sailing: how to raise, lower, and trim the sails, read the weather, steer a course, and maneuver the boat in and out of a slip. But sailing is also about feel. Over time, one develops a relationship with the boat. One feels it, has faith in it, and most importantly, learns to have faith in one's self.

The same is true for pursuing dreams.

A WIND SHIFT

*A*s the pendulum of corporate life swings from centralization to decentralization, acquisition to divestiture, differentiated product margins to commodity pricing, jobs are frequently added and subtracted. Lives hang suspended, like weights on a grandfather clock, awaiting the tolling chimes of change.

Three times in my tenure with the company, my job has been eliminated. With the support of mentors, I have always found other positions, other opportunities to broaden and expand my experiences while remaining with the company.

This time, I am the one recommending the job go away. Given the organizational changes necessary in 2004, the decentralization of the company, the thousands who are losing jobs, and the changing landscape of healthcare delivery in the United States, I believe it is the right thing to do.

"The position is one the company can no longer afford," I explain to my boss, the chairman and CEO of the company that has been my employer for more than two decades. I respect this man and feel fortunate to represent a company whose products save people's lives. But this time, I am not planning on searching for another position within the company. This time, I am prepared to walk away and start over.

At least I think I am ready.

There is a side of me that is terrified of life without a paycheck. Memories of my struggles in Africa cloud my view of the spread-sheets littering the top of Rubin's and my dining-room table.

"You should be fine," our financial planner assures us. But the worrier inside me is not convinced. What if the market crashes? What about medical emergencies? What about unexpected surprises? What if we run out of money when we are too old to find jobs?

"We can always find jobs, Mary," Rubin says softly.

The deluge of logic that has controlled my decisions for decades showers me with its familiar arguments. But another voice is emerging, one that refuses to be silenced.

How do I know this is still my life's work? What if there is something else waiting for me, something I cannot uncover while engrossed in an all-consuming career? What if I have accomplished and learned all that I need on this path? What if I am placing money above that which God would have me do with the second half of my life? What has happened to the writer? To the one who lived to be outdoors? What if I am meant to pursue my dreams?

Writing the word "Faith" on a ceramic tile I place on the corner of my desk at home, I leave the roster of employees in December of 2004. I am fifty-two years old.

The only certainty in my life—in our lives—is the overwhelming need to live near the eastern shores of Lake Michigan. When I close my eyes to envision our future together, I see the seemingly infinite silver-blue sheet of water, edged with the whitecaps of the wind; I hear it rolling against a sandy shore, smell the freshness of life defined by its presence. A childlike excitement surges through me, and I find myself smiling without thinking.

Until I start thinking.

The unfamiliar blank calendar on my wall is daunting. The lack of purpose in my life spins an unexpected web of dread into my days. Rubin quickly settles into engineering and building a myriad of projects for our new home in West Michigan, our boat, and the homes and boats of our friends. But I struggle. I know I am meant to do something with the second half of my life, but what?

I walk the beach daily, looking for an answer.

Most of the time, the lake's surface is defined by southwesterly winds. Depending on the wind's velocity, the water rolls and heaves, splashing and crashing against the sand. But when the wind whispers from the east, the lake laps quietly at my side, sheltered by the massive sand dunes towering above me. Looking west, I can see the dark shadows of the wind's footprints skipping merrily across the lake to the other side. But beside me, the lake is a mirror for the wispy, white clouds floating across the sky.

Sanderlings, tiny beach scavengers with long black beaks, scurry along the water's edge, hurrying to keep ahead of me but hesitant to miss a single morsel. Seagulls soar and squawk overhead. Occasionally, the black head of a cormorant pokes above water, surveying life briefly before again diving below to catch its next meal.

Soft, white sand and ever-shifting dunes define this side of Lake Michigan. I've lived on the other side, experienced life along the severe, rocky shoreline. After a lifetime dominated by my left brain, by a career defined by results spewing from a calculator, I came here to rediscover my right brain, the artistic side. Something tells me it is hidden somewhere just below the sand.

My job is to find it.

SQUANDERING GOLD

*F*or years, I have come to this lake to bask in its beauty, to bow respectfully to its seemingly infinite power. I have stood before it with my heart open, prayers flowing as freely as the sunlight skipping across its surface.

Not today.

Standing in the bow of our sailboat as a light wind propels us forward, I stare at the murky waters of Lake Michigan. It has been days since torrential rains overwhelmed antiquated sewage systems and spilled millions of gallons of raw sewage into this lake, since swollen rivers and creeks flushed phosphorus-rich soil, fertilizers, debris, and other contaminants into these waters. It seems as if the silvery-blue hue defining the lake's surface has been permanently replaced with a filthy shade of brown.

I feel the anger bubbling inside me. I want to blame someone, to point the finger angrily at those responsible. How could they let this happen? Why don't they fix the sewage systems? Why don't they clean up the rivers and harbors flowing into this lake? Don't they know this is our drinking water? Don't they know we can live without a lot of things, but clean water is not one of them?

The internal chatter stops abruptly.

Spilling out of a crevice of my mind like a rain-swollen river is the long-buried memory of a twenty-two-year-old woman standing on the side of a road, willing to risk everything for a drink of water. I remember my shame, my anger, my overwhelming sense of helplessness. Above all, I remember that jug of water clutched in my sweaty hands.

Staring at the grungy waters of Lake Michigan, something shifts inside me. For decades, I have muffled my own voice behind the political correctness of neutrality I felt integral to my career. No more. I am going to channel the passion I feel for this lake, the anger that we are polluting it, into a voice calling for change. This is my home, our home. We must do a better job caring for it, protecting it.

But first, I need the facts.

"The ecosystem of the Great Lakes is at a tipping point," a scientist explains to the several hundred of us crowded into the pews of the Fountain Street Church in Grand Rapids, Michigan, several months later. "If steps are not taken immediately, damage to twenty percent of the world's fresh surface water could be irreversible."

My eyes wander upwards, drawn by the eleven stained glass windows reflecting the waning light of evening skies. The terminology is unfamiliar, but the message is clear. The influx of aquatic invasive species, the frequency of sewage overflows, toxic pollutants such as mercury, the presence of PCBs (polychlorinated biphenyl) and pesticides in nearby soils, the loss of wetlands and other coastal habitat, the absence of consistent reporting methodology, and the lack of sustainable approaches to development have placed the lakes in grave danger.

In stark contrast to the aura of tranquility usually found in a historic church laden with the work of artistic masters, I am irritated as I listen to the team of scientists, engineers, business leaders, and representatives for tribes and government agencies, commissioned by President George W. Bush to assess the ecosystem of the Great Lakes. How could this happen?

Closing my eyes, I see myself standing before Lake Michigan when hurt and sorrow whip through me like gale-force winds churning the deepest waters of my heart, when options stretch before me like grains of sand, neither black nor white, but thousands of tormenting possibilities painted in infinite shades of brown. With my feet grounded in sand, my hair tossed by the wind, my ears soothed by the rhythmic sound of waves, I am no longer afraid. I feel Lake Michigan before me, sense its power, its ability to adjust to the ever-shifting forces of weather and seasons. Its many moods mirror my own. In its presence, I feel strong, connected to a force far greater than myself.

Quietly retracing my steps to the entrance of the church, I fill out a card, adding my name to the list of those wishing to speak at the 2005 public hearing conducted by the Great Lakes Regional Collaboration. I cannot remain silent.

"My husband and I are newcomers to Western Michigan," I explain when my name is called and I've threaded my way to the podium edging the giant stage. "We recently moved here from Nashville, Tennessee. Our neighbors in Tennessee thought we were crazy. 'People don't move north for the second half of their lives,' we were told repeatedly."

I hear people chuckling in the audience.

"My husband and I have traveled all across this country. We could have lived anywhere. We opted to move here because of Lake Michigan. We have lived in communities where fresh water is scarce, where summer droughts limit water availability. And while we can live without a lot of things, clean, fresh water is not one of them."

As an executive of a Fortune 500 company for more than two decades, I was accustomed to addressing large audiences, familiar with boardrooms paneled in cherry, steeped with history, rich in ambiance. But never have I delivered an impromptu speech where my voice was as clear, my passion as resolute, as this evening, when I stand on stage before a crowded church, talking about the lake of my childhood.

Congressman Vernon Ehlers, Republican Representative from the 3rd District, is in attendance for the entire hearing. An ardent supporter of the Great Lakes, he voices his commitment to crafting and introducing bipartisan legislation designed to implement the recommendations of the Collaboration. After the hearing, I work my way into the crowd of people surrounding him, determined to say thank you.

"You should run for office," he replies. "You're bright, articulate, and clearly passionate about the Great Lakes."

Surprised at his suggestion, I smile and say, "Thank you." But his comment weighs heavily in the recesses of my mind, creeping to the surface as I struggle to define my life's purpose. While running for political office does not feel right, I have a responsibility to do something. But what? Without being affiliated with a giant corporation, I feel naked, inadequate.

What can I possibly do to help?

CAN ONE PERSON MAKE
A DIFFERENCE?

"Do you know your face lights up every time you talk about the Great Lakes?" Alene Moris asks. Known internationally for her work with women on career and leadership issues, Alene is counseling me on how I can use my talents in the second half of my life.

I look at her quizzically. Since returning from the public hearing in Grand Rapids, I have been studying the Great Lakes Regional Collaboration report, learning about the eight key stressors threatening the health of the lakes, sharing my findings with friends, neighbors, and now Alene.

"Why not write about what you are learning?" Her eyes crinkle as she smiles, her energy and passion for life erasing any hint of her eighty years.

I can think of many reasons why it is not a good idea. I am not a journalist. I am not a scientist. I have no credibility. Why would anyone want to read, much less publish, my work?

"You are responsible for your efforts on this earth, not necessarily the results," she continues, as if reading my mind.

But publishing also allows others a doorway into that part of self I protect. I risk judgment and criticism. And while I am accustomed to the rigor of an annual 360-degree feedback process in my former work life, this is different.

Writing is a reflection of a part of me not tapped since youth. It is the essence of a long-buried dream.

My heart racing with nervous anxiety, I contact the editorial-page editor for the daily newspaper, *The Holland Sentinel.* To my surprise, he invites me to write a monthly opinion column.

"Faith is a bird that feels dawn breaking and sings while it is still dark," Alene assures me. "When you are on the right path, doors will open for you."

If I am going to be a student of faith, to trust in the force that prompted me to leave a successful career, to believe in a dream, I need courage to walk through those doors. I have to overcome my fear of failure and disapproval.

And I need to invest in a dictionary and thesaurus.

Seven months later, in September of 2006, in a convention hall in Cleveland, Ohio, at the second annual Healing Our Waters Great Lakes Coalition conference, I listen surprised and dumbfounded as the opening speaker reads an essay I know by heart.

CAN ONE PERSON MAKE A DIFFERENCE?

This morning, like most mornings, I ran inland for roughly an hour. It is part of my daily ritual, providing me time to reflect, to meditate, and, of course, to sweat.

My cool-down walk along the shores of Lake Michigan is my treat to myself. My heart sings when I see this magnificent body of fresh water, touch its soft white-sand beaches that stretch for miles, and look up at the towering dunes steadied by strong, tall maples, oaks, and pine trees. This is sacred space.

Yet, scientists say it is in danger—the ecosystem of the Great Lakes threatened with irreversible damage if something is not done immediately. I shake my head in disbelief. How could this happen? More importantly, how do we reverse the slide?

The challenges facing the Great Lakes are daunting, so overwhelming it is easy to feel powerless as an individual. I have lived my adult life in corporate America, most recently in a position reporting to the CEO of one of the largest healthcare manufacturers in the world. I know nothing about getting involved as an individual—without the backing of a $10 billion corporation and the support of millions of people.

Even so, I know I cannot remain silent. While I have traveled to places of spectacular beauty, none touch me like the Great Lakes. In my heart, these waters are home.

So, I talk about the Great Lakes and all I am learning.

In the process, I have discovered I am not alone in my passion for protecting these great waters. Neighbors, family, friends—even those who live outside the region—are interested in understanding the past decisions that have brought us to this tipping point and the tradeoffs needed in finding solutions. Almost always, the first question someone asks me is: "What can I do?"

It is the same question I ask myself during my early morning runs. Over the years, I have found if I can still the constant chatter of my mind as I run in the first light of sunrise, answers to the toughest questions often surface.

I ask, "What can I do to protect these waters I love?" The answer seems obvious. Get educated, energized, and engaged. No problem with the first two. It is engagement that holds the most uncertainty.

"You are responsible for your efforts on this earth, not necessarily the results," a friend tells me.

And so I have embarked on a journey of faith, taking one step at a time. For me, the first step is to begin writing.

And this essay, my first, posted on the Internet, picked up by the Director of the Great Lakes for the Sierra Club, and shared with a coalition that would grow to more than 145 zoos, aquariums, museums, and conservation, outdoor-recreation, and environmental organizations, is the beginning. What I did not realize is that just as one must chart a zigzag course to reach a destination that is into the wind, I would need to change tacks many times on my journey to protect the lakes so integral to our lives, so easy to take for granted.

"DON'T LET IT FLY"

*T*he waves, fueled by westerly winds, spew frothy waters toward my buried feet. Scanning the horizon, I see the wind knocking the tops off the waves, shimmering slivers against the blue. Whitecaps mean it is blowing at least fifteen knots, I think automatically, trained by Rubin to read the water.

A lazy smile touches my face as I listen to each wave roll along the shore, fading in the distance as the next wave crashes nearby.

Surely life cannot get any better.

The screeching call of a seagull overhead breaks my trance. Slowly, I pull a trash bag from my pocket and begin walking south, heading toward the entrance to the Kalamazoo River. This morning my mind drifts to the upcoming talk I am to give the fourth-grade classes at Quincy Elementary School. The last time I was in a fourth-grade classroom was as a fourth-grader.

When teachers Kathy Nemeth and Donna Altman first approached me about speaking to their classes about the Great Lakes, I jumped at the chance. Protecting these waters is a passion, and writing the monthly newspaper columns has given me access to the world of science behind the necessary restoration. But what will resonate with fourth-graders?

A man with leathery brown skin eyes me as I near his lawn chair on the beach.

"I hope someone is paying you," he says, pointing to the trash bag.

Surprised by his comment, I stop.

"I've waited my entire life to live by the water," I reply. "I feel like it's the least I can do."

He and his wife say nothing.

"And besides," I add, "the walk is good for my body. Picking up trash is good for my soul."

And then it dawns on me. I know exactly what to talk about!

▲ ▲ ▲

The students stare in amazement as I dump a large bag of trash collected from the beach onto the classroom floor.

"Oooh, gross," are the first words spilling out as they plug their noses and eye the pile of litter.

"Where did all those balloon ribbons come from?" someone asks.

I say nothing, watching the kids survey a floor littered with bottle caps, candy wrappers, straws, and plastic containers. Heaped in the center of the pile is a giant mountain of ribbons tied to remnants of balloons. The mound reminds me of a volcano with thin strips of colorful lava flowing in all directions.

"I never thought of balloons as trash," a voice pipes up.

"Me, either," pipes another.

"Most people don't think of balloons as trash," I say. "So what could you do to inform people? To let them know? So when you visit the beach, there are not so many balloon ribbons littering the sand?"

"Pick up balloons we see on the beach and put them in the trash," exclaims one.

"Not let go of balloons," several shout simultaneously.

The class promises to do both.

"What else?" The faces look puzzled. "Do you think other people consider balloons trash?" I prompt. "What if we created a multimedia campaign to educate people? What kinds of things could we do?"

"Make posters to put in the hallway."

"Do a skit for the school."

"Pass out flyers in our neighborhoods."

"Take a field trip to the beach, and pick up balloons."

Each idea sparks another, like tiny flames in a firepit of dry twigs.

"Make T-shirts."

"Create a movie."

"Yeah! Create a movie!"

"Put signs in the windows of stores selling balloons."

I write furiously on flip charts, racing to keep up, determined to capture every idea.

"We can write letters to the editor."

"And send them to newspapers in Wisconsin and Illinois," a little boy says knowingly. "We have to let the people on the other side of the lake know because the winds come out of the west and blow their balloons on our beaches!"

Soon the classroom blackboards are wallpapered with sheets of paper reflecting the creative exuberance of the fourth-graders.

Orange dots become ballots to mark favorite ideas, to prioritize the campaign's efforts.

"Every good campaign needs a slogan," I tell them.

Theirs is perfect. *Don't let it fly, or the Great Lakes will cry.*

Armed with a slogan, passion, intensity, and dogged determination, the students spend the next several weeks blanketing the community with their message. When they learn two local high schools are planning to release hundreds of balloons at the upcoming graduation ceremonies, they invite the principals to visit their classroom.

Sandy balloon ribbons are stacked in a heaping pile in the corner of the classroom, the result of a field trip to Saugatuck State Park. Above the pile, a photograph of a fish skeleton entangled in a long, black balloon ribbon is taped to the wall. Evidence.

The students, like diplomats, plead their case, imploring the principals to have the senior classes throw beach balls in the air, release bubbles or butterflies. Anything but balloons.

The orders totaling 450 balloons for the Zeeland High Schools are canceled.

When I feel overwhelmed and discouraged at the seeming lack of progress in the cleanup of the lakes, I head to the beach, trash bag in hand. As my footprints zigzag across the sand picking up the flecks of distracting color, I think about the sparkling faces of the forty-two fourth-graders, eyes filled with hope and endless possibilities. I cannot let them down. I will not let them down.

Eight years later, the students would graduate from Zeeland High Schools in ceremonies that remain balloon-free. They are my heroes in a world where heroes can often be hard to find.

SEEKING COMMON GROUND

"Why are there two bottles of rum in the cockpit?" I ask. Sweat is rolling down my face as I pause in the midst of vigorously scrubbing the boat.

Rubin is strolling leisurely down our pier, hands in his coat pockets, blue eyes sparkling, a good-natured smile stretched across his face. I can tell, even without asking, he's been wandering about the marina kibitzing with everyone he knows. Which is everyone.

"I'm not sure."

"Hmmm."

"I didn't think you'd be back from running this soon," he says, stepping from the dock to the boat. "I would have cleaned it."

"Hmmm." I swallow my skepticism. The white fiberglass is splattered with tiny specks of blue spider droppings and splats of brown-crusted bird poop. It is not the kind of filth easily erased by the expensive, environmentally friendly cleaners I use. Rubin's solution is to use tire spray, bleach mixed with a commercial boat wash, Soft Scrub®, and toilet-bowl cleaner. They work.

"You can't use those! All that toxic stuff goes straight into the lake!" But I have no facts to influence change, just hunches. And hunches, in our family, don't count for much. But I suspect we boaters have a lot to do with the quality of water in our harbors based on how we paint the hulls, treat our gray water and bilges, and fuel and clean our boats.

"I love nature, provided it doesn't invade my castle," Rubin says frequently. And whether his castle is on land or water, he is equally passionate when it involves insects.

On the boat, it starts with spiders. At the first hint of dusk, they emerge, weaving misty webs from all corners of the boat. Rubin's solution is to go on "spider patrol," a nightly ritual in which he grabs a flashlight and a giant can of insecticide and sprays anything that moves on the stanchions, lifelines, boom, side stays, dock lines, pier, or electrical box. If he has enough poison, he sprays the neighbors' docks and electrical boxes as well, creating a long death march to our boat.

A two-inch perimeter around our house is treated in a similar fashion. I'm lucky it's only two inches.

"You must have been buried alive in a prior life," I joke, trying to be empathetic by adding humor. But the more I learn about ecosystems, about nature's way of providing balance, the more I realize insects are a vital part of life. And while I would prefer they live elsewhere, spiders, in particular, seem to have a strong affinity toward docks, lines, and boats.

It is the poison I most abhor. And so on mornings like this one, I search for the live, balled-up spiders and bugs above the droppings and squish them before rinsing their bodies into the lake. Fish food, I tell myself. Not the perfect compromise, but a beginning.

Often the bugs escape Rubin, the spiders, and me but drown in the heavy dew of morning. Barn swallows flit about the boat, scooping up the leftover bugs for breakfast, reminding those paying attention—like me—that nature does provide its own cleanup. Unfortunately, the swallows tend to perch on the boat's lifelines, digesting their meal and pooping leftover remnants all over the fiberglass. Rubin tries to deter the birds by tooling about in our dinghy when I'm not around, destroying the first hint of any nest under nearby docks.

"There are plenty of places they can build their nests," he tells me. "Just not here."

The birds don't seem to care. Like insects, they are relentless, partying on any boat with bugs. And, occasionally, that includes ours.

This morning's scrubbing is a ploy. If I want to spend hours hunched over a brush trying to clean the boat with environmentally friendly cleaners, I can do so. He has better ways to spend his time.

"So what's with the rum?" I ask again.

"I think they might be gifts."

"Why?"

"For using the slingshot to chase the cormorants off our neighbors' boats."

"Are you kidding?"

"Those birds consume copious amounts of fish during the day. If they perch on your mast during the night, the boom is covered with a thick, brownish poop-soup. You can't get it off."

Silence.

"Anyway, you'd be proud of me."

"Why is that?"

"I used acorns to hit them. Environmentally friendly."

"Thanks."

THE STERN HEAD

"Is it okay if I use the stern head?" a friend asks. His face is serious, but is he?

I glance over at Rubin. Everyone who knows me has heard my spiel at least once, most likely several times. I am passionate about updating the antiquated sewage systems dumping millions of gallons of raw sewage into the Great Lakes during heavy rains. I advocate publicly for the prioritization of local, state, and federal dollars to finance new facilities, which would separate sewage systems from storm runoff to minimize the spills.

"We can live without a lot of things; clean, fresh water is not one of them," I say to anyone and everyone willing to listen. My enthusiasm makes me an easy target to tease, so I don't know. Is he serious? Is he really asking if it's okay to pee off the back of our boat?

The weight of responsibility for cleaning up Lake Michigan sits heavily on my shoulders. I know it is not coincidence that the universe has steered me north to a home near this lake. And yet, I am discouraged. I have poured my energies into writing columns and giving presentations on the need to restore and protect the Great Lakes. I've watched former Steelcase CEO, Peter Wege, and the Wege Foundation pull together leaders of zoos, aquariums, environmental, conservation, fishing, and hunting organizations to create the Healing Our Waters Great Lakes Coalition. Rather than taking a splintered approach to obtaining necessary legislation and funding for the initiatives outlined in the 2005 Great Lakes Regional Collaboration report, the coalition has created one massive, powerful lobbying voice. It should be a voice difficult to ignore.

And yet, it seems so little happens. From afar, the lakes look clear and pristine. People do not see their restoration as a pressing issue. As a country, we tend to wait until things become a crisis before we act. Like Hurricane Katrina. In 2005, Katrina ripped through New Orleans, eventually costing taxpayers more than $122 billion in repairs. The cost to human lives is incalculable. And yet, much of the damage could have been avoided if Congress had ratified and funded the 1998 plan to redesign the levees. The plan was shelved because of its $14 billion price tag. I fear our Congressional leaders will ignore the Great Lakes, just as they ignored the levees. And with each passing year, the $20 billion cost of restoration increases as preventative measures are ignored and damaging pollutants mushroom in scope and severity. At some point, the damage will be irreparable.

If our friend is serious, I don't know what to say. Admittedly, I, too, have peed and puked in these waters. But that's before I knew better, before I understood the fragility of the lake's ecosystem. He and I both know we do not share the same values regarding the environment. The intellectual side of me says no one on our boat is ever going to pour human waste directly into this lake. The emotional, anything-for-a-friend side says maybe it's okay this one time. Surely, he is just giving me a hard time.

"You know," our friend continues, "my using the stern head is nothing, compared to all the sewage dumped by the big cities into this lake."

He is serious.

I want to say everyone can help; everyone can do little things to make a difference. And if we start with even the smallest of steps, the distance grows shorter and the bigger steps easier. But I realize others do not share my beliefs or sense of urgency, certainly not our friend. I fear too much passion spoken too frequently dulls the message, or worse, drives a wedge between the very people who must find ways to live alongside each other respectfully and peacefully, while sharing limited resources. I am working hard on smoothing the intensity of my message, on listening more carefully to the views of others. But the little voice inside me weeps at the thought of allowing someone to pee from the very boat that has reconnected me to this lake.

The swirling dilemma chews up at most twenty seconds. Rubin turns to look at me, and I detect an inkling of a smile.

"Did you know most people found drowned in Lake Michigan had their flies open?" he says.

We all laugh, and our friend climbs down the companionway to the head, tucked just off the main cabin, to relieve his bladder.

MOTOR GUY

*G*lassy waters stretch in all directions as the sails flap listlessly in the muggy air. There is no sound, except the clanking of blocks as the headsail swings lazily from one side of the mast to the other, void of air. The morning sun sparkles against the pale blue water, a lovely sight were it not for the steamy heat sucking the energy from the air and all life save the flies.

Perched in my customary spot behind the wheel, I sit with arms wrapped around my knees, heels tucked closely to my body. My cheekbone rests on my wrist as I stare at the chalky gray line dividing the lake from a cloudless sky. If I crank my head hard toward the east, I can just barely see the tips of the dunes, tiny islands floating in the distance. Ten miles would be my guess, for Rubin says we lose sight of land at fifteen miles out.

Closing my eyes, I wait for his voice from the cabin below. Waiting is almost always better than worrying. And with the boat's motor malfunctioning, I could spin myself into a dizzying swirl of anxiety.

Relax, I tell myself. At least he's good with motors.

I remember the first time we went car shopping, roughly six months after we were married. Rubin's excitement was that of a child ripping apart the Christmas wrapping of a giant gift from Santa. "Look at that high-tech dashboard! Check out the rims of those tires! Can you see the sleek design and great aerodynamics? What do you think?"

I didn't want to admit I had quit thinking hours earlier. I was exhausted. If I had any thought, it was that I couldn't believe we'd spent a gorgeous autumn afternoon trekking to every car dealership within a sixty-mile radius to find me a new car. I abhor shopping, all shopping. The most despised, however, is car shopping.

To Rubin, the only thing better than shopping for cars is shopping for boats. There is a thrill associated with researching the latest technology, investigating the endless possibilities. For most of our married life, the mailbox has been stuffed with magazines like *Road & Track, Motor Trend, Sail, Yachting, Cruising World*. He can spend weeks investigating a potential purchase and never tire of chatting with knowledgeable salespeople, forever in pursuit of the best deal.

When we finally arrived home from the extensive but unsuccessful search for my new car, I flopped wearily into a chair. Pulling two sheets of paper from a nearby drawer, I said, "You list your top criteria for buying a car. I'll list mine."

His list: Is it unique? Does it make heads turn? Is it fun to drive? Does it have a high-performance engine? My list: Reliable. Durable. Dependable. Preferably more than one drink holder.

"A car is transportation," I tried to explain. "It gets a person from Point A to Point B." Even now, Rubin cringes when I utter what he considers a nonsensical statement. And so I did what any young woman would do who is vested in a relationship. I relinquished all responsibility for cars. The one caveat: "The car better work every time I turn the key."

In hindsight, it was brilliant. I don't do oil changes, rotate tires, talk to mechanics, and only on rare occasions, do I confer with a car salesman. I put fuel in the car. Occasionally, I help wash it, albeit begrudgingly. I remember living in Columbus, Ohio, and golfing at a local country club. Both cars happened to be filthy, so I bet Rubin closest to the pin on a par-three hole that the loser would be responsible for cleaning both vehicles. Several hours later, he was sticking his hands in a bucket of soapy water.

I missed a hole-in-one by less than an inch!

▲ ▲ ▲

For most of the thirty-plus years of our marriage, the vehicles have functioned perfectly. When I think back, only two cars really tested him. One died on the Tri-State during rush hour traffic as I wildly dashed to catch the last flight home to Nashville. Stranded a few miles from O'Hare in a drenching rainstorm on a Friday evening, I angrily stewed while repeatedly calling and listening to a busy signal from the Chicago branch of AAA. Finally, I hung up and called the guy in charge. Not calmly, I admit. Not without a few expletives. But even Rubin, who patched a phone call from the Nashville AAA to the Chicago AAA and ultimately back to me, could not get a tow truck there immediately. I was stuck.

To his credit, Rubin diagnosed the problem as a damaged water pump and encouraged me to start the car again in ten minutes, after the engine cooled. The Eagle Vision chokingly turned over and limped through a tollbooth, a parking gate, and halfway into a parking spot before dying. By the time I arrived at the airport, the flight was gone. Rerouted through St. Louis on an extremely tight connection, I again missed the flight to Nashville, spending the night in a St. Louis airport hotel with only a computer, a notebook, and a Palm Pilot. No toothbrush. No deodorant. No comfortable clothes. Nothing.

I never touched the wheel of that car again.

The other vehicle to constantly challenge our early pact is his baby, a 1997 Corvette. Most of the time, it stays in a neighbor's garage, "increasing in value." According to Rubin, the Corvette is "an investment in a different bank." The lower the mileage, the better the investment. I quit trying to talk sense into him long ago.

When it works, it is a very fun car to drive. It's at its orneriest when I am alone behind the wheel, like the time it refused to shift into reverse at a bank parking lot in Nashville. Another time, red lights flashed across the dashboard before the engine shut down at an intersection across from Nashville's busiest shopping center. It turned out that the tires needed air. And there was the time the passenger-seat window refused to budge, remaining partially open as rain splattered wildly across its black leather seats. More than any other car we've owned, the silver Corvette reflects some creative, fiercely independent, feisty, and fun-loving streak running through Rubin. But it is not his favorite. That title goes to his first car, the one he bought when he turned eighteen, a 1952 MG.

He tells me it never worked.

I place motors in the same category as cars. Not my thing. This one, the one that powers our boat when there is no air, has sputtered and stopped ten miles into a ninety-mile crossing of Lake Michigan—a crossing I swore I'd never do again. Flicking a pestering fly off my leg, I wait for Rubin's curly head of hair to pop up from the cabin. And while it's a blessing we're not crossing in a violent storm, if the wind doesn't build, it's going to be a long day.

The morning drags into midday. An errant ripple of water thumps lightly against the hull, rousing me from a dreamy, sun-induced trance. In my mind, I know the sun's rays can be deadly, but my body relishes the warmth wrapped about me. There is a fluidity of life flowing through me, a sleepy tranquility as I drift with the boat on placid waters.

"Turn the key." Rubin's voice from the cabin startles me, and immediately my head jerks up. In the cockpit, I switch the key to start the motor, and a warning siren shrieks from the speaker in the engine control panel, shattering the silence. I race to pull the engine shutoff button, to return the key to the off position, to restore quiet to the morning air. I hear the shuffling of tools and the muted sounds of Rubin, the mechanic and guy in charge, in the engine compartment below, trying to find the fix to the motor's piercing cries.

A few moments pass, and I hear: "Try again."

The alarm again explodes in the hushed cockpit, its desperate wail as grating as fingernails dragged against an old-fashioned chalkboard. Again, I scramble to turn everything off, to restore the calm. While I cannot see his face, I sense Rubin's frustration and try to remember something about motoring the last five to six miles that may help him discover a cure. For, while I don't care about cars, I care deeply about this boat that has accompanied me on so many emotional, physical, and spiritual journeys. I know this boat, feel this boat. What is wrong?

A half-hour clicks by, maybe more. It reminds me of sitting on a chair next to a hospital bed, waiting for a diagnosis for my dad, unsure whether to be mildly concerned or genuinely frightened. Nervous acid begins gnawing the inner lining of my stomach. What will we do if he cannot repair the engine?

"Found it!" A hand appears from the dark of the companionway, fingers clutching a small, silver basket, brimming with slimy weeds that dribble pea-green water on the white fiberglass deck. "We must have picked this up while in the Ludington harbor."

Sweat mats his usually tousled hair, and his face is flushed with the heat of working in the cramped engine compartment below. He swirls his forefinger around the basket to clear the lake weeds from the silver mesh. Always a teacher, he begins explaining: "This is the basket which filters lake water used to cool the engine. When it gets clogged, the engine overheats and stops. Like now."

Beaming and obviously relieved to have discovered the source of the problem, he dumps the stringy green weeds, resembling seaweed, overboard before heading down to replace the basket. "Okay, try again," he hollers a few minutes later.

The key clicks, and the deafening alarm again sends me rushing. "How can that be?" I cry, anxiety creeping into my voice. He does not answer, for he does not know. The silence, treasured earlier, creates lines of worry, boring into the skin between my eyebrows.

The increasing presence of lake weeds and algae in Lake Michigan and its harbors is troubling. I wrote a column for *The Holland Sentinel* expressing alarm at the death of thousands of birds, their bodies littering the beaches of Sleeping Bear Dunes. Behind the poisoning are two of the issues outlined in the Great Lakes Restoration Collaboration strategy for cleaning up the lakes: the influx of aquatic invasive species like quagga and zebra mussels, and pollution caused by rainfall and snowmelt picking up contaminants from the ground as the excess flows into rivers, streams, and lakes. Contaminants include fertilizers and pesticides from agricultural runoff, and oil, gasoline, and grease from roads, parking lots, and driveways.

According to scientists, the invasive quagga and zebra mussels, now prevalent across the region, filter the lake water, allowing sunlight to penetrate deep below the surface. The sun's rays, combined with excessive levels of phosphorus and fertilizers contained in surface runoff, fuel the growth of algae. Scientists suspect one possible culprit responsible for the death of the birds is the explosive growth of native algae, cladophora. The dense green mats of the algae form an ideal breeding ground for avian botulism, a poison they suspect is infiltrating the food chain from plankton, to fish, to birds, including loons.

Alone in a tent in Sleeping Bear Dunes National Lakeshore a short while back, I heard the wail of a loon, an eerie three-note cry that floated across the quiet campground. Instinctively, I held my breath, waiting in anticipation for its mate to reply. Silence. Only silence. Until the air escaping my lungs created a long, heart-breaking sigh. All I could see were beaches strewn with dead birds, including my beloved loons.

While the stainless steel basket contains a common lake algae, not cladophora, the weed's rapid growth and increasing density fueled by the clearer waters and high levels of nutrients flowing into the harbors is problematic. Nature out of balance is good for no one.

I swat at the biting flies flocking to our fiberglass island in the middle of the lake. They dart away momentarily before landing again, inches from my body. I grab a flyswatter and smash it against the deck. They scatter, untouched. And return. After a while, Rubin reappears. In his hand is a coat hanger and another heaping mound of the weeds.

"They actually clogged the water intake hose leading from the lake to the basket," he says, shaking his head in disbelief. "I had to thread this hanger through the angles in the hose to get them out. But I think I've got them this time. Try the engine."

I turn the key, and the deep rumble of a motor responds. When I catch his eye, I kiss my pointer finger and stretch it toward him—our private code for "Thank you, I love you—you are my hero."

We motor-sail to Sheboygan without interruption, except for the flies. By the time we arrive, he has spent the day wielding a flyswatter in one hand, a can of insect repellent in the other. The cockpit is littered with tiny black corpses. And while there are days I advocate for the fly—for the role of insects in nature's circle of balance—that is not today. Today I am rooting for the motor guy.

OPEN TO CHANGE: 2008–2012

When the lake is a sheet of glass without a breeze to darken its surface, one can wait patiently for a shift in the weather . . . or one can turn on the motor.

Sometimes one must be open to change.

LISTENING TO THE RIGHT SIDE
OF MY BRAIN

Should I camp alone? Is it safe? Is it crazy? Can I even do it? The idea defies logic. It challenges the rational left side of my brain. And yet, I'm driving a car crammed with an odd assortment of camping gear. On the passenger seat, a map of Indiana is folded so that the large green area titled "Indiana Dunes National Lakeshore" is clearly visible.

The inside of the car is silent. No radio, no book on tape. In stark contrast, the voice inside my head has not stopped chattering since I left Western Michigan earlier in the week. I realize I have been anguishing over this decision since the idea surfaced several months ago. The questions pit logic against emotion.

Is it safe for a woman to camp alone?

It has been decades since I smelled the thick smoke of a campfire, heard the crackling of wood, felt the warmth of the fire penetrate the leather of my boots. I can still taste the gooey-sweet marshmallows and warm, silky chocolate, squashed between two graham crackers. I remember snuggling deep inside a down-filled sleeping bag, only the tip of my nose touching the brisk night air.

Part of me longs for the opportunity to camp again. Part of me is terrified.

My ever-rational, always-controlling mind agrees with family and friends. It is a ridiculous idea. But months ago, when the trees outside my window still bore a light dusting of snow, my close friend, Tracy, asked me what I was doing to honor the voice that speaks gently to me in dreams.

"You have always let that strong voice of responsibility govern your life," she said with great compassion. "What are you doing to honor your heart's voice?"

Stunned, I thought about her question as I jogged through darkened streets, watching the first hint of sunlight transform the blackened canvas around me to silhouettes of maple, oak, and sassafras trees. When the answer came to me, it was clear and shocking.

You have sailed these great waters, gazed in wonder at the towering sand dunes edging the shoreline, felt drawn to the seemingly wild, mysterious life of the forests. You have experienced Lake Michigan from the water. Why not explore it from land? Why not go camping?

Camping?

"My idea of camping is a Holiday Inn," Rubin told me early in our dating relationship. At the time, I didn't bother to dig into the details. In hindsight, I think it had something to do with mosquitoes, spiders, ants, and other insects potentially creeping into the tent, invading his space.

But for me, camping has been magical since my childhood. A part of me longs to reconnect with the ruggedness of outdoor living. I suspect it is the creative, free-spirited voice of the right brain, that same voice that urged me to quit writing the monthly newspaper columns, an all-consuming, left-brain journalistic style of writing grounded in science. Perhaps the universe has something in store for me that I will never experience if I do not learn to listen, to take risks, to balance the voice of my right brain with that of my left.

So, with a mixture of childlike excitement and adult-like trepidation, I began assembling my hodgepodge collection of camping gear that had survived our many moves across the country. Missing were the obvious: my warm sleeping bag and the accompanying pad to keep me off the chilly ground. Once I discovered a frayed, intact cotton sleeping bag in the garage and an unfamiliar, unused, very old, four-man dome tent, I figured I could survive anything. If other critical items were missing, I could always run to the store. At least, that was my plan.

I'll camp in Manistee, I decided, remembering my first experience with family at Orchard Beach State Park. Then a phone call from my mother changed things. Instead, I drove to St. Louis, joining her for the funeral of her oldest brother. Studying the highway maps from Michigan to Missouri, I noticed a patch of green depicting the Indiana Dunes National Lakeshore, a national park extending along the southern end of Lake Michigan.

Perfect. I'll stop on my way home and hike the spider web of trails forking through the Indiana Dunes. I jammed the trunk of my car with camping equipment, but the internal debate continued for the seven-hour drive to St. Louis, reconvening as I began the trek north.

Is this wise? If it's such a great idea, why doesn't anyone else think so? I can almost see my blood-splattered body on television, read the headlines "Woman raped, strangled, butchered while camping alone." *Who would pity a woman so irresponsible? Maybe it is a nutty idea.*

The exit sign for the Indiana Dunes National Lakeshore looms before me. *Okay, I won't camp this trip—I'll just gather information,* I tell myself, pulling off the highway. Stepping into the visitor center, I note its cleanliness, feel its warmth, its welcoming appearance.

Surely, this is a good sign.

"We've never had any issues at our campground," an official-looking park ranger tells me after I spend a half-hour getting briefed on the many hiking trails available along the shore.

"There's a host living at the campsite who keeps an eye on things," he continues. "A park ranger drives through periodically. And besides, the Beverly Shores police are right across the street. They keep a pretty tight rein on things in the area."

I feel my confidence rising slightly.

If I just drive through the campground and check it out, I'll know immediately if it's the right thing to do. I don't want to live a life controlled by fear. Wasn't that my motto as a youth? Never look back and wish I had done something. I've always thrived on adventure, tackled far more dangerous feats. I can do this. I want to do this. I have to try.

My stomach in knots, I ignore the entrance ramp to the highway home and follow the signs to the campground.

The retirement home Rubin and I share in Michigan is like a tree house. During the summer, every window overlooks the lush green forest of the backdunes. If I look closely through the heavy canopy of leaves, I can see the distant blue of Lake Michigan, hear the rhythmic sound of the waves washing against the shore. At the first hint of morning, chickadees, cardinals, sparrows, and woodpeckers greet me. At night I can hear the rustle of deer, possum, raccoons.

The large bay window in my office overlooks a steep, narrow valley threading through the mountains of sand to the lake. Outdoor decks grace all three floors of the Victorian house, providing the perfect spot from which to write. Less than a block away, miles of sandy beach await my footsteps.

I live in the woods, in the dunes, near the lake. And here I am, driving toward a campground in the woods, in the dunes, near the lake, but parallel to the daily commuter trains to Chicago.

Maybe I am crazy. Will I be safe? Why am I doing this?

THE WHISPERS OF WILDFLOWERS

*T*his is not the door I imagined opening when I began re-creating my life.

Dressed in my hiking attire—a pair of ragged olive pants, a black-and-maroon-checked flannel shirt, scuffed leather boots, and a suede mesh hat hanging around my neck—I eye the audience of roughly sixty people, the majority of them my age.

I am recounting a story I have told to garden clubs, nature groups, park visitors, assisted-living facilities, and women's organizations across Western Michigan. This afternoon, I am the featured speaker at the spring wildflower sale at the Gillette Visitor Center in P. J. Hoffmaster State Park. Taking a deep breath, I begin.

"I remember that first night lying on the frozen earth, teeth chattering, eyes wide, listening to Lake Michigan's icy winds whistle through empty branches. My body trembled, partially because of April's arctic air expanding and collapsing the flimsy walls of an old nylon tent and partially because I was a fifty-six-year-old woman alone in an empty campground after midnight.

"What I hope to share with you are the three things I learned on this journey hiking, biking, and camping alone up the eastern coast of Lake Michigan. First, losing the role that has dominated one's life for decades can actually be a good thing. Second, finding answers to life's swirling questions, to that chattering of mind that can be all consuming, requires stopping, becoming fully present. Lastly, the questions we choose to pursue should be selected carefully, mindfully. For seeking the answers often defines our lives.

"When we first moved to Michigan in 2005, I never noticed wildflowers. Like many women in their mid-fifties, I raced through life, trying to balance my role as wife, daughter, sister, friend, and corporate executive. I was a president for a Fortune 500 company, responsible for creating and maintaining relationships with hospital executives across the country. I lived in four- and five-star hotels where I could wrap myself in a soft, oversized white robe, with ample amenities in a bathroom several steps away, and only a phone call needed to get a cup of hot coffee delivered to my room.

"My calendar crammed with activities, I ignored the voice whispering to me as I jogged in the early light of dawn, urging me to slow down and reexamine the priorities in my life. One day, I decided to listen, to walk away from a successful business career and reinvent the second half of my life. My only certainty in this quest for purpose was the overwhelming need to live near the eastern shores of Lake Michigan.

"Our Nashville neighbors thought us crazy. 'People don't move north for the second half of their lives,' we were told repeatedly. But as avid sailors who had sailed three of the five Great Lakes, my husband and I had fallen in love with the waters of Lake

Michigan, the rolling hills of sand and miles of beaches defining her eastern coast.

"This journey up the coast from the Indiana Dunes to Sleeping Bear began as a quest for answers to questions created by time, created when the role previously dominating my life disappeared."

I pause briefly, remembering that tumultuous time in my life.

"I once read that life's transitions are like the trees. In the autumn months, the leaves fall to the ground. No matter how hard we try to place them back on the branches overhead, they remain on the earth's floor. We cannot go back. Winter follows, with its cold, gray days, a time of deep soul-searching and painful self-examination. The darkness is difficult but necessary for spring to finally unfold. [2]

"'What does your heart want?' a dear friend asked me. Pondering her question in my early morning run, I heard the answer immediately, and it was shocking. 'Go camping.'

"My husband, Rubin, is a boataholic. When I first met him more than thirty years ago, he made it very clear his idea of camping was a Holiday Inn. So this notion of going camping came out of nowhere. As for gear, it was nonexistent. But I decided to scrape together whatever I could find and set off alone to discover the dunes ... and myself.

"Packing my car with a tent, a hodgepodge of old gear, and a bicycle, I set off in April. In Tennessee, April is spring. April in Michigan, I was to learn, is borderline arctic."

I notice lots of smiles, a few chuckles.

"I remember the evening I told my husband of my decision to go camping. Other men would have vehemently protested the absurdity of a decision so risky. But Rubin listened quietly, honoring the untraditional voice of his wife, a woman wrapped in question marks. Before I backed my car out of the driveway, he handed me a parting gift. A sack of weapons."

The audience laughs.

"Inside the cloth pouch was a canister of pepper spray (which, if I pulled it out in the middle of the night, I'd undoubtedly point in the wrong direction and spray myself); a whistle (a good idea if there had been another person in the campground; there wasn't, not in April); and a knife (which is an accident waiting to happen in the kitchen, much less a tent.). So while it didn't make me feel any safer, I loved looking at the pile heaped on the floor of the tent each night and feeling my husband's presence.

"Not surprising, the transition from luxury hotels like the Ritz-Carlton to a tent initially was a lesson in survival. But I did survive and miraculously figured out how to pitch an old-fashioned, complicated dome tent. Not without lots of attempts, more than a few expletives, and a little help from the wind. But I did it, repeatedly, as I moved up the coast."

More than a few heads nod with knowing smiles, and I realize I'm not the only one who has wrestled with poles, tarps, and stakes that stubbornly refuse to cooperate.

"I froze, of course, for I never noticed the absence of leaf buds on the branches of the bushes and trees surrounding the campsite. For the first several weeks, I was alone. But as my journey headed north and the weather warmed slightly, I met other campers willing to share their knowledge, experience, and recommendations regarding gear with a woman sitting on the edge of a picnic table with a laptop, feet perched on a firepit ring, a starter log for a fire."

Once again, a few chuckles rippled through the room.

"My days were spent climbing steep, forested backdunes, mountains of sand often 200 feet high. Heading toward the lake, I wandered through the interdunal troughs and across the foredunes, rolling hills of sand peppered with dune grass. Eventually I reached miles of flat, sandy beaches. On and on I marched, until I could no longer run away from . . . or to . . . anything . . . until I just stopped.

"And looked around.

"And saw the wildflowers poking their faces through the drab remnants of winter. They had been there all along, just waiting to be noticed. Hoping to learn their names, I paused to take their photographs so I could scour wildflower books in the evening by the campfire, so I could greet my companions by name the next morning. Photographing the flowers meant I was squatting, kneeling, often crawling along the earth's floors to capture every detail of these unique little treasures.

"I learned to see through the lens of my camera.

"And it was as if the seed of an artist, long buried beneath a left-brain perspective, began sprouting roots . . . as if the wildflowers were whispering the lyrics to accompany the music of my heart . . . providing the very answers I was seeking.

"I started writing stories inspired by the wildflowers, each written in exactly one hundred words, combining the passions of my heart with the disciplined rigor of limiting verbiage. In hindsight, the self-imposed one-hundred-word mandate bridged a thirty-year career focused on analytical, left-brain activities with this new heartfelt voice unleashed by the discovery of nature's treasures.

"I'd like to read to you one of the stories from my book, *Tiny Treasures: Discoveries Made Along the Lake Michigan Coast*. It is titled 'Nature's Encore' and was inspired by the trilliums I found in what is called Giants' Valley, the home of the last remaining white cedar forest in Michigan. It is located on South Manitou Island, part of the Sleeping Bear Dunes National Lakeshore.

NATURE'S ENCORE

It would take three of me, arms outstretched, to hug the girth of a gnarly cedar marking the entrance to Giants' Valley. In the shadows, troupes of floppy white Trilliums gather, dancing wildly, celebrating spring.

Hiking quickly, I barely notice.

Shyly peeking her head from beneath a wide, green umbrella, the bell-shaped face of the Nodding Trillium stops me.

"What is your hurry?"

Embarrassed, I kneel to photograph the graceful bodies performing to the music of the southwesterly winds. As if in appreciation, the rare face of a Red Trillium peers around a downed giant, smiling for the camera."[3]

Of all the photographs I share with the audience, the ones showcasing the delicate beauty of the Large-flowered, Nodding, and Red Trilliums are my favorite. I wait a few seconds, giving the audience time to savor these unusual wildflowers, and then continue.

"Initially, I photographed every flower, in the belief that all flowers are created equal. I learned, however, there are some that are transplants to our region, invasive flowers that actually harm the environment, our health, even our economy. After a neighbor planted her dune with crown vetch, one of the fastest-spreading and most invasive plants, I decided to go on a campaign and do my best to educate people about the plants that are harmful to the area. A list of invasive plants can be found in my book. It's my way of ensuring that the little native traveling companions I met are there for future wanderers.

"When I left the company, a dear friend and mentor told me, 'Faith is a bird that feels dawn breaking and sings while it is still dark.' I now know who I am and what I am meant to do with this time of my life. Through my writing, photography, and public speaking, I advocate for protecting home: the waters of Lake Michigan stretching to our west; a coastline boasting the world's largest freshwater sand dunes; the trees, birds, butterflies, wildflowers, and all with whom we share this sacred place. This is home. And home is worth protecting.

"I learned there is really only one question—for me—worth asking: How do I reflect the thumbprint of light placed on my soul at birth? Seeking that answer changes everything.

"When clouds of mist fog my mind, confusion muddles my vision, or tears of pain run down my face, I disappear into the closest patch of wilderness searching for wildflowers, or slide behind the wheel of a sailboat, or jog a frozen beach. Immersed in nature, I see my priorities change, ideas magically appear, the intensity of the current issue dissolves, and I am at peace.

"As you share in my writing, photography, and public speaking, I hope you feel the same."

Greeting me when I finish the talk is the man who is always there, arms outstretched, helping to open the doors I choose to walk through . . .

Provided there are no bugs.

WINTER WALKS

"The only people who live north in the winter are people who have never lived south," Rubin tells the world when gale-force winds sweep across the lake, snow stinging the eyes of anyone walking on the beach.

That, of course, would be me.

Occasionally, Rubin joins me as I explore a world barely visible through the sheets of white, hiding a path I know by heart. The lake, I have learned, always dances in harmony with the wind. Most winter days, it moves slowly, rocking to a melancholy rhythm as if it, too, is chilled by the wintry air. But when fierce winds whip across its surface, the lake responds as if in anger. Fueled by its massive size and depth, its rage boils into frothing waves, splintering the ice and hurling chunks on land. The smaller pieces shatter, the larger ones remain, slowly morphing into an icy mountain, mirroring in size the dunes to the east.

My path weaves blindly between the walls of white.

A rogue wave forces its way under the ice mountain, blasting a hole through the top, searching for freedom. A fountain of water sprays the air as the lake reminds all of its mighty power. The mountain shudders. A sheet of thin ice cracks, rumbling and breaking the snowy silence.

When pressed, I struggle to name my favorite season, each so different in defining beauty. For me, the excitement is in the transition: the hushed green blanket of the Dutchman's Breeches spreading across wrinkled layers of leaves; the first bits of human chatter emerging from shuttered cottages near our home; my mother's favorite shades of gold and orange splashing the dense foliage overhead; the first snowflake to touch my tongue. Nature's transitions create a restlessness within me, spark a longing to explore, an awareness that my time on earth is limited.

And so I wander, the artist within me fully engaged. With a camera slung around my neck, I search for treasures.

I am never disappointed.

WHY I NO LONGER RACE

I am afraid. Not for me, for we are securely tied in a spider web of lines at the White Lake Yacht Club, just north of Muskegon, Michigan. But though it is after midnight, I sit on the first step of our boat's companionway and stare at the northern skies. With each bolt of lightning slicing the wall of blackness and rumbling the thick, muggy air, I shudder. On such a night, no one should be on this lake. And yet they are. Thousands of "Mac" racers are most likely sandwiched between Sleeping Bear Dunes and the Manitou Islands, a perilous stretch of Lake Michigan under which many shipwrecked boats lie buried in the sand. The racers are scurrying to get sails lowered, praying lightning does not strike, hoping the storm blows through quickly.

In my mind's eye, I see the smiling faces from this afternoon as we sailed through the fleet of sailboats racing in the Chicago Yacht Club's race to Mackinac Island. It was a perfect day for the famous race—steady air from the southwest, sunny skies. Billowing spinnakers in an array of cheerful colors dotted the skies as boats skimmed across the water.

"Thanks!" the Mac racers shouted as we repeatedly changed tacks to ensure we did not affect their wind.

"Good luck!" we shouted back. "Be safe!"

In exchanging those few words, I connected with this year's racers in a way I have not since Rubin raced the Chicago to Mackinac in 1982. Now, twenty-nine years later, I can picture the hooded bodies huddled over the rail with heads down, wind and rain pummeling their faces as the icy spray from Lake Michigan douses them. With every strike of lightning, I think of the hundreds of masts—lightning rods—moving slowly with sails stowed on deck, the boats powered only by the wind against those masts, and perhaps, a handkerchief of a headsail.

"Mary, are you guys buttoned up?" I hear the concerned voice of a neighboring boater walking down the dock. "I've been on the phone with the Mac racers. The storm is moving our way, and it is huge. One of the Mac boats is over, several people are in the water. They are trying to find them . . ."[4]

It is a recurring nightmare. A wave breaks over my head, and I resurface, gasping for air. The shocking coldness of the water sucks the air from my lungs. I tread frantically at first, trying to pull my shoes off while keeping my head above water. And then I move slowly as the numbing begins. I fight the fear of aloneness in the blackness of the storm. Wave after wave washes over me. And then, just once, my timing is off, and water floods into my nose and mouth. I begin sinking . . .

I remember my last race on a monohull. It was more than thirty years ago, while Rubin and I were still dating. I agreed to be a substitute on an O'Day 27, racing with Rubin during one of the regularly scheduled long-distance regattas sponsored by the Bay City Yacht Club on Saginaw Bay.

"Take the helm!" shouted Tom, the owner and captain of the boat, before dashing up to the foredeck.

"But I've never been . . ." My voice tapered off as I grabbed the tiller and stood alone in the cockpit, ". . . at the helm."

The wind screamed through the rigging, filling the giant spinnaker, and rolling the boat on its side. Water rushed along the toe rail, and it felt as if we were capsizing, as if the keel was lying flat against the surface of the water, as if we were inches from being pitched over the side and into the swirling fury of Lake Huron.

And then the gust vanished, and the boat snapped up. Momentarily. The next blast of air slammed it back down, and the seemingly endless cycle of terror began again. Voices were yelling from all directions. I heard them shouting in the bow as they tried to wrestle the spinnaker from the clutches of the wind. Off the stern, I heard people hollering as the spinnaker of another boat bore down on us. The mark was dead ahead, and yet the boat below us appeared to be taking us up, forcing us either into the mark or crushing us into the other boat. It seemed as if people were shouting at me to do something, and yet I had no space in which to maneuver. My fingers gripped the tiller to inch the boat up slightly. Nothing happened.

"Rubin," I called out, "what do I do?" My panicked voice disappeared into a crescendo of rushing water, clanking halyards, hollering voices, and the ominous sound of the wind filling the giant, colorful spinnakers surrounding me.

"Here, I got it," a tall, good-looking man, responsible for trimming the main sheet, took the tiller. I clambered to the rail on the windward side, hoping my weight would help offset the wind. "Railmeat." That's what I had been told I would be today—just dangling my feet over the high side.

Our spinnaker was finally down, and I saw the boat on our left, on the windward side, pulling ahead and out of harm's way. Later, I would learn our boat "broached," a term meaning "the uncontrolled turning of a vessel so that the hull is broadside to the seas."[5] When that happens, steering is impossible. By placing me at the helm, Tom knew I had something to hold on to, that I would not be plunged into Lake Huron, that I would be safe.

What I realized that afternoon as I shivered on the rail, more from fear than cold, was that I did not want that kind of relationship with nature. And while storms were an inevitable part of sailing, I did not want to increase the odds of running afoul of these lakes by religiously crossing a starting line regardless of conditions. While I would continue to race on the Hobie Cat, I would not race on someone else's boat. At least with Rubin, I had a chance to talk reason into the competitive spirit of a racer.

Now, as I stare at the night skies and repeat prayer after prayer for the downed racers—for those possibly living my worst nightmare—I know I made the right decision to quit racing. Rubin continues to race on others' boats. But not tonight. This stormy night, he is asleep in the aft cabin. Safe.

And for that, I say a passionate prayer of thanksgiving.

DESTINATION PORTS

"We can get you a new one," Rubin says, trying to be helpful. "It's not that expensive."

I am frantically scurrying about the boat, rummaging through duffels, scouring every pocket and nook in which my favorite running watch might be hiding. It's not the money that's troubling me, it's losing the familiar. It took forever, but I can finally set the alarm and adjust the time on my first attempt. Rubin, gifted with an ability to quickly analyze mechanics and fix anything, would be mystified that my shoulders sink with despair at the thought of learning a new watch.

"I'll just call the marina and see if it's been turned in," I finally reply. "I probably left it in the shower."

We left port more than an hour ago, as dawn lightly brushed the skies over Leland Harbor and the northeast tip of Lake Michigan. The odds of finding the watch are not good, but I have to try. I remember Rubin hailing the marina several days earlier as winds knocked our sailboat on its side and rain pelted us with an intensity that felt as if millions of needles were jabbing every sliver of exposed skin.

"Technically, we aren't allowed to take a reservation until you actually pull into the harbor," the harbormaster said, with empathy in his voice. "But we have several slips available at the moment. And don't worry, we'll find a spot for you somewhere. We won't turn you back out in this weather."

I could have hugged him. If anyone can find my watch, it will be him.

"No. No one has turned anything in," a woman on his staff replies when I call. "I'll tell you what. Give me your number, and I'll go check the showers and call you back."

I am flabbergasted at her offer and tell her so. It is a long walk from the fuel dock to the showers. She shrugs it off, and five minutes later, the cell phone rings. "The watch was right there on the bench," she reports.

"Thank goodness!" My relief is obvious. "I know it's an inconvenience, but can I give you a credit card to pay for an envelope and postage and have you mail it to our house? Please? I would so appreciate it. Add an extra $20 for a tip."

I hear Rubin mumbling in the background. "The watch is worth only fifteen dollars."

"Of course, we'll mail it to you," she says. "But don't worry about the credit card. We'll take care of it. No problem."

The watch beats me home, and Leland tops my list of favorite destination ports.

According to a 2007 report released by the Great Lakes Commission, vacationing owners of boats of more than forty feet spend an average $275 per day in a harbor community and $76 if the boat is less than sixteen feet. The money is spent on dockage, fuel, food, drinks, gifts, clothing, souvenirs, and, most important, boat supplies.[6] (The boat of a boataholic, like Rubin, wants for nothing.)

What makes a destination port, a place in which boaters choose to spend their time and money?

Provided the channel is deep enough that our keel does not bounce off the bottom and wide enough that a storm surge does not roll us against the break wall, the marina forms our first impression. We want to tie up to a dock that is maintained: solid—not tipsy—when we climb off the boat; secure pilings on which to tie lines. We want to feel safe from storms, protected from possible theft or vandalism. And the facilities must be clean. Spotless is better.

Rubin, the chef in the family, prefers a grocery store within walking distance, grills, picnic tables, and an assortment of affordable and fun bars and restaurants. But he's also favorably impressed when dockhands know how to correctly cleat a boat, can assist transient boaters docking in the midst of a storm, and know the true depth of the water they oversee.

To me, a destination port is about the people. All I am looking for is a smile, a touch of kindness. And because that powerful human trait is contagious, no matter how exhausted I feel as we motor into a harbor, no matter how stiff, bruised, and weather-battered, I must remember that the circle of kindness begins with me.

TELLTALE SIGNS

Sailing the wilderness of the North Channel is something I have wanted to do for decades. But unlike other vacations, Rubin and I did not negotiate or trade anything. It is his unspoken gift to me, a gift to heal a shattered heart.

In hindsight, the signs of vascular dementia in my dad were as clear as the wildly fluttering telltales of an untrimmed headsail. I should have known, despite my dad's bulldog determination to die in his sleep at home, despite my mother's unwavering resolve to care for her husband "until death do us part," there are some decisions over which we have no control. The inevitable process of aging is one of them.

But I was clueless and therefore totally unprepared.

This trip is like a lifebuoy flung to one sinking slowly beneath the crushing weight of responsibility for making heartbreaking decisions involving the care of others. For after watching dementia squeeze the oxygen from the brilliant mind of my dad, stripping him of the ability to think, reason, or remember; after feeling the brunt of his dementia-fueled rage and paranoia; after holding the hand of my mother as grief plunged her into an unfamiliar pool of darkness and despair, I am empty.

After many months in Arizona with my parents, Rubin's gift will bring light, laughter, and adventure back into my life. And ours. And because it is a sailing trip, it starts, of course, with the adventure.

THE HARBOR LIGHT

A gust of wind, invisible save its shadow, sweeps across Lake Michigan, darkening a surface already heaving from the storm. Glancing to my side, I see the next wave bearing down on us, towering over our forty-foot sailboat. In seconds, it rolls underneath the hull, lifting the boat momentarily before plunging us into the trough. The sails start to flutter a warning. The wave is pulling us too far off the wind, threatening to jibe the boat and fling the boom to the other side. If that happens, the sheer force of twenty-eight-knot winds grabbing the sail as the boom flies across the cockpit could sever the mast.

Frantically, I muscle the wheel to pull us back on course. And then the gust slams into the sails, yanking the boat up into its clutches, up to where it threatens to suck the air from the sails and stall the boat. I turn the wheel hard in the other direction.

One hour into a seven-hour journey, my arms ache as I referee these two powerful forces of nature, wind and waves. Even after Rubin reefs the headsail, making it smaller, I am overpowered. I don't want to voice what I feel—that with each roar of the wind, each wildly frothing wave spilling alongside our boat, I am afraid.

Rubin takes the wheel, and something about the grim intensity on his face sends me scrambling down the companionway to get the radio. "How does this work? I know I say 'Mayday,' but how do I turn it on? And tell me again what I do if you go overboard." I realize I should not wait until a crisis to review safety protocol, but I never think about it during leisurely sails.

My tailbone on the edge of the seat, I sit with knees straight and toes pressed against the other side of the cockpit. With one arm wrapped tightly around the winch and the other hand clutching the teak seat, I feel as if I am perpendicular to the water, staring at the waves. "Should we be tethered?" It is my last question, and it brings a pause. I know he is scrolling through his card catalog of articles on the pros and cons of tethering.

"No," he replies slowly. "The water temperature is sixty-two degrees. We are maybe three miles from land, and the waves will sweep us to shore. We're better off floating freely in the water than to risk getting caught under the boat."

Intellectually, I know our boat is designed for this type of weather, that I am safe. Emotionally, I am not convinced. Between gusts, I anxiously scan the distant horizon, skies the color of dirty cotton balls etched in metal-gray. If I can just see the thin silhouette of the Ludington harbor light, I know we will be okay, I tell myself.

On calm days, particularly when seeing them backlit by a sky streaked in the soft pastels of sunrise or the flaming shades of sunset, I find lighthouses and harbor lights romantic. Not today. Today is about survival. I am looking for that towering structure of cement, steel, stone, and iron, constructed to withstand the indifference of nature, designed to guide weather-battered boaters, like us, to safe harbor.

Once on land, with my feet firmly planted in the sand, I promise to photograph this harbor light that withstands the merciless pounding of wind and waves. For like the wildflowers that edge the wetlands or dot the forest in spring, this light reminds me to pause and be grateful for every moment of life.

SEARCHING FOR THE SWEET SPOT

*T*his morning, she is like glass, a sheet of crystal twinkling in sun's early light as we leave Ludington on this journey north along the coast of Lake Michigan and then eventually east, across Lake Huron, through the North Channel, and into Georgian Bay. Lake Michigan's tranquility mirrors my own. I feel the slight kiss of the wind on my cheek and notice pockets of air beginning to skip lightly across her surface.

"When sailing in light air, avoid the holes, the flat patches on the lake's surface," Rubin has told me. "Sail for the ripples, the darker spots on the water."

I have learned to love the ripples.

My feet rest on the bottom of the wheel, guiding the boat. My hands are wrapped around a warm mug of coffee until I begin talking. Then, mug secured in a nearby drink holder, my hands sweep across the air like a paintbrush on canvas, coloring my words with their movements.

"Hands," is what my mother's twin brother calls me. "If we tied up your hands, you couldn't talk." He laughs.

It's true.

My feet feel the breeze pulling the boat to weather and automatically turn the wheel a sliver off wind. In light to medium air, I have sailed the boat with my feet as long as I can remember. I find it easier to feel the collective forces of nature on the boat. I tend to be more patient, less apt to take control, and more willing to wait for the boat to find its own equilibrium. My feet tweak direction rather than overpower the wheel. Arms free, I can lean back against a cushion strung through the stern rail and eye the compass, making slight adjustments to keep us on course. Occasionally, I'll lean over the side and check the telltales on the headsail.

It is, unquestionably, my favorite method of steering.

"Pay attention—they're gaining on us."

"What?" I spin around, scanning the horizon. "I thought this was a leisurely sail," as if there is such a thing when another sailboat is anywhere within sight.

Rubin cranks the headsail in slightly, moves the traveler, and tightens the mainsheet to get perfect shape in the sails.

"Watch your telltales."

"I am." Both hands now on the wheel, I dutifully check the telltales, eye the wind indicator above the mast, double-check the compass, and glance back at our competitor. If the sails are trimmed correctly on a course heading, the boat almost sails itself.

I lean back, feet on the wheel. Sail trim is Rubin's job.

Today's destination is Frankfort, Michigan. My heart skips with joy as I scan the coastline, just north of Ludington. As we work our way around Big Sable Point, home to Ludington State Park,

I look for that spot on the ridge where I once felt the exuberance of spring flowing from every pore in my body.

I recall leaning against a tree on the highest point of the Ridge Trail and seeing my beloved lake framed by black branches, still sparsely clothed with the first hint of buds. Tall clumps of beach grass the color of winter wheat swayed in the breeze as spring tiptoed across the rolling hills of sand, dusting the grass with splashes of green. Scrappy Jack Pines darkened the narrow valleys paralleling the lake. Buried in the deepest hollows of these interdunal troughs were Ludington's jewels, unexpected and breathtaking freshwater ponds, teeming with life.

To the east, through the crimson buds of the red oaks and slivers of maple leaves just beginning to unfurl, I saw the brilliant turquoise of Hamlin Lake. Everywhere I looked, spring's magical wand was sprinkling the earthy browns with hints of color. I remember an overwhelming sense of gratitude radiating from within me, like streaks of sunlight emanating from beneath a thin bank of clouds.

At that moment, I suddenly realized how one-sided my relationship was with nature. I was euphoric in her presence yet knew so little. Intimacy, life touching the deepest part of my heart, required knowing, understanding, and caring. It was, I realized, why I became informed and engaged in addressing the issues plaguing Lake Michigan. The same should hold true for all life along her shores. They, too, opened me to God.

Now, seeing the dunes from the water, it rekindles the wonder of that moment and brings clarity to all I have been learning.

From the water, you can clearly see the blowouts, U-shaped areas of open, shifting sand, typically found in the parabolic dunes shaping the southeastern corner of the lake. Void of vegetation, blowouts form when high lake levels and strong, westerly winds destabilize the sandy dunes. Over time, beach grass and other vegetation root along the edges of the blowout, forcing the sand up. The result is the formation of dunes, often soaring as high as three hundred feet.

The shoreline changes as we sail north, nearing Manistee. The dunes are replaced with giant bluffs of moraine, a mixture of sand, gravel, silt, and clay deposited by glaciers formed centuries ago. The cliffs are darker, more rugged-looking than the white sandy dunes shaping the coast from Michigan City to Ludington. By the time we reach Sleeping Bear Dunes National Lakeshore, just north of Frankfort, we see what are called perched dunes. These are created when the lake erodes and destabilizes the bluffs, whisking the loose sand up the face of the bluff and depositing it on top. While the cliffs look massive from the water, the actual dune itself is much smaller than the parabolic dunes to the south.[7]

"I'd really like to sail the coastline of Indiana sometime."

Rubin says nothing.

The Indiana Dunes are considered linear dunes, formed from the irregular cycles of high and low water levels. Defined by wet marshlands and long, parallel ridges of sand, the dunes are located in overlapping ecological transition zones. As a result, the area is a resting spot for more than 350 species of migrating birds and home to 1,135 different native plants and a rich assortment of other wildlife. I have spent days roaming the trails that thread through the area, photographing the diverse assortment of plants and wildlife. But it is one of the few places on the lake I have not seen from the water.

"Do you think we could sail there sometime?" He still doesn't answer. I know he is not enamored with the ports on the southern end of the lake. My guess is I'll have to negotiate a trade.

"The wind is building," Rubin interrupts my thoughts.

The glassy surface is now rolling with one- to two-footers. The wind is pulling me to weather, toward the west. The waves are pushing me toward shore, east. Wind and waves vie for control. East. West. Left brain. Right brain. The writing. The photography. The science. The art.

My job is to search for the balance, so that I fight neither; I tap the strength of both ends of the spectrum. In the equilibrium, the sweet spot, a gentle tug on the wheel in either direction triggers the power of nature to keep me on course.

My legs, strong running legs, are perfect for the job. Only later do I realize how much I have been taking those legs for granted.

RITUALS

"Mary, our boat is not really equipped for wilderness camping."

"Why? What do you mean?"

"We don't have a generator, a large enough holding tank for the head, a windless system to hoist the anchor line . . ."

He went on for several minutes. I thought it an excuse. After all, the trip to the North Channel involved sailing and motoring around hundreds of remote, uninhabited islands, anchoring in deserted coves, exploring and photographing life on the islands. A wilderness that raw would most certainly attract bugs. And it would take at least a month. He would miss almost an entire season of racing.

I couldn't imagine his resistance was truly about our boat until he began preparing for the trip. It took weeks, multiple trips to West Marine, Menards, Lowe's, Eldean Shipyard, Wolf's Marine, and several thousand dollars spent on boat additions and modifications.

I truly had no idea. "What kinds of things are you doing?"

"Well, if we're going to anchor, we have to have more chain to keep us from drifting and a longer, heavier anchor line. I've got to buy backup batteries for the motor, at least three. We'll need to update the GPS chips, buy nautical charts and a Lake Huron port handbook. We won't be able to sail that far with *Indy*; she's too heavy and bulky. I'll have to buy another inflatable that weighs less to get us to shore. And that means designing some kind of system on the stern, so we can mount it—not drag it in the water."

"Can I help?"

"Not really. I'll have to add a section of hose to the handheld sprayer in the head, so we can shower in the cockpit. But I guess the most important and time-consuming task is designing a system so we can have coffee in the morning and a hot meal in the afternoon."

"What do other boats do?"

"True cruising boats have generators that provide power while anchoring."

"Can't we just buy one?"

"There is no place for a generator. Our boat is designed as part cruiser, part racer. Space is limited. I don't have any place to put it."

"Oh."

I haven't always been a coffee drinker. Actually, Rubin introduced me to it one frosty September morning when we were sailing the San Juan Islands. I saw him walking down the pier at Friday Harbor with two large Styrofoam cups.

"You know I don't drink coffee!" My foul-humored bark was edged with the misty cold weather that had kept my lips trembling for what felt like an eternity. "I haven't touched coffee since college.

It ripped my stomach apart right before my final exam in statistics. I barely made it through."

"Just drink it," he said good-naturedly. Nothing ever rattled this man.

"Mmmmm. What is it?"

"Coffee and Baileys."

"Oh."

I've been a coffee drinker ever since, eventually eliminating the caloric, alcoholic, and potentially addictive Baileys. I substitute cream. But it has become a morning ritual, one we share together at daybreak before parting to go our distinctively different ways.

Preserving the ritual on our trip to the North Channel is proving almost impossible. After weeks of research, he reconfigures a small cabinet adjacent to the galley and mounts yet another battery with something called a sine wave inverter.

"It takes the DC power and modifies it so an AC appliance, like the coffeepot or microwave, can work off the battery."

"I have no idea what you just said, but it sounds good."

For the first week of the trip, we have warmed leftover pizza and hot dogs while under sail. But about the time we reach the remote islands of Canada, where generating power is critical, the system shuts down.

"What did you do?" he calls down from the cockpit. A buzzing alarm is reverberating from the cabinet, shattering the romantic peace of the morning.

"I don't know. I just flipped the switch on for the coffeepot, which, by the way, is not working. Looks like it's dead."

For the next several days, as we sail through the most pristine waters I have ever seen, Rubin works in the cabin, trying to find answers. He uses longer cables to reach the heavier batteries, testing to see if the malfunction is in the batteries or the inverter. He reads and rereads the inverter instructions to see if he has configured something incorrectly. I stay at the helm, trying to focus on the beauty and serenity of the water, basking in the warmth of the sun, photographing the hundreds of birds flying and diving nearby.

The evening of the third day without power, without coffee, without a warm meal, Rubin says it is my decision.

Looking at the GPS chart on the pedestal, I see we are less than one nautical mile from a decision point. One option is to anchor at Eagle Island, an island friends say is a favorite, that's reported to have blueberries ripe for the picking. The other option is to sail another four hours to Little Current, a port with a marina, a place where we have access to electricity, a place we can get a cup of hot coffee.

"What's our food status?" I ask, for Rubin—not I—provisioned the boat.

I hear what I suspected.

"Same as yesterday, and the day before. Peanut butter and jelly sandwiches, a few slices of ham, and lots of cheese, crackers, and nuts."

All his creative energy that went into purchasing soups, chili, trail meals, and food that could be heated by microwave when at anchor was for naught. I am torn. Not only are we without rations, but anchoring is hard on him. I watch his back and shoulders strain as he pulls up the heavy chain and anchor each morning. I'm inclined to keep sailing, to head for Little Current.

"I don't know. I miss the ritual of coffee with you in the morning. Maybe I'm getting too old for this rugged camping style of life."

After a few minutes, he says quietly, "We'll sail to Eagle Island."

That afternoon he rows me to shore where I photograph wild irises, bullfrogs, herons, and the pinkish rock that defines so many of the islands in the region. We scour the shrubs for blueberries to no avail. It is too early in the season.

The next morning, after our shower in the cockpit, Rubin suggests I start the engine. I do, without thinking much of it, and watch a family of ducks paddling nearby, five feathery ducklings under the watchful eye of the female. After a bit, Rubin's curly-haired head emerges. In his hands are two cups of steaming hot coffee.

"Good morning, beautiful," he says, with a grin as he inches over to sit next to me in the cockpit. "It dawned on me while showering that I could use the power cables to jury-rig the engine's battery to the inverter, so I could make us a pot of coffee."

Once again, I have no idea what he is talking about. But the cup of coffee is delicious, the reintroduction of the ritual, even better.

BUD

"I will not hurt you, little one," I say softly to the dark eyes peering at me above the water. The wet, whiskered nose is in the air, the small round ears flattened to the sides of its head. Most of the long, chocolate-colored body is submerged as it glides effortlessly through the water.

Quietly, I pull the lens cap off, click the camera on, and begin focusing on the animal swimming toward me. It's not a fancy camera, just a simple point-and-shoot. But it has taught me what it means to be fully present, to be so immersed in nature that I am one with the subject I am trying to photograph. When this camera is hanging from my neck, I notice the little things: the fluorescent turquoise of the damselflies' hair-thin bodies flitting among the reeds, the bulging eyes of a curious bullfrog peering at me from the shallows, the opaque wings of two dragonflies mating on a speckled boulder near shore. With each click of the camera, I am overwhelmed with the beauty found in nature, humbled by the diversity of creation, grateful to be alive. No matter where I am, when I pause and take the lens cap off, I am a different person.

I am the person I want to be every minute of every day.

The beaver dives, the splash of his tail breaking the hush of early dawn. Drifting in a small, inflatable dinghy in Covered Portage Cove in the North Channel, I see our boat anchored in the distance, its stark white hull providing contrast to the muted blues of water and sky. The cliffs towering above the cove are softened by hundreds of fir trees, jutting through cracks in the rock. Near shore, a blue heron stands erect, all neck and legs camouflaged in the same palette of grays, silvers, and peach as the boulders creating the platform on which it stands. A dark navy stripe runs along the top of his beak above his eyes and then splays out like two wispy thin braids of hair behind his head. He stares intently at the water below.

The beaver resurfaces closer to the dinghy in which I sit and slaps its tail against the water before immediately diving again.

"I won't hurt you," I repeat. But the beaver is not listening, clearly agitated. Its eyes are pleading every time it surfaces, as if trying desperately to communicate. It stays only a moment before dousing the air with droplets and disappearing beneath the clear, cold water.

"Oh, you have a nest nearby." I finally understand its message. Placing the cap back on my camera, I pick up the oars and row silently away. Nature will provide an encore elsewhere. It always does when I choose to be present.

Bud, a chalky-colored eight-foot inflatable dinghy, is the newest addition to our fleet. Its name is printed in royal blue letters on a flashy yellow nameplate placed on the transom where motors usually are mounted. Unlike our previous three inflatable dinghies, *Bud* slides through the water powered by muscle, not motor.

Our first dinghy, purchased as an anchoring companion for our sailboat, *The Inevitable,* Rubin called *"The Boat."*

"It's a perfect day for *The Boat,*" he'd say when giant swells transformed Lake Michigan into an apparent ocean. Young, crazy, seemingly indestructible, we'd skim perilously along the crest of waves in *The Boat,* the bow suspended out over the water. As a wave began losing speed, we'd plunge into the trough below. The stress of this sport we called "wave-hopping" eventually splintered *The Boat's* wooden floorboards. We were fortunate not to have shattered our spines.

The next dinghy was upgraded to metal floorboards. Named *Indestructible,* or *"Indy"* for short, its life ended when age cracked the rubber around the seals and the inflatable pontoons began leaking air. By the time we bought *Indy II,* a rigid-bottom inflatable dinghy, I no longer had any interest in having my body jarred and jolted by high-speed jaunts across a rolling lake. Even so, Rubin placed a twenty-horsepower motor on the new eleven-foot dinghy.

"Why?" I asked.

"It's the maximum size available."

"Of course."

Indy II is perfect for cocktail cruises with friends. However, it is too big and bulky for me to singlehandedly lower it into the water to go exploring, camera in hand. And while Rubin can start the motor with one swift yank, my arm feels as if it will fall off before I usually flood the engine and give up. For this excursion into the wilderness of the North Channel, *Indy II* is too heavy to tow behind the sailboat.

Bud was my birthday gift to Rubin for me. For while he may have selected the name and mounted it on the stern of our sailboat, this lightweight dinghy with two oars and a rubber floor has "me" written all over it.

"HOME, JAMES"

With a six-and-a-half-foot cast-iron keel lurking below the water line, do we thread the narrow passage between islands or turn around and sail the longer, deeper, safer route through the northern edge of Georgian Bay to reach Killarney, Ontario?

My eyes dart from the compass to the GPS four-color screen mounted on the pedestal in front of me to the depth sounder displayed near the companionway. Standing on the steps leading to the cabin, Rubin hunches over his new iPad, studying the navigation application. Below deck, a parallel ruler lies on top of charts scattered across the table of the main cabin.

The answer depends on which of these sources of information is the most accurate.

I remember the first time we crossed the ninety-mile width of Lake Michigan in our thirty-foot Catalina. For ten of the thirteen hours, we could not see land. Rubin spent most of the trip below, charts stretched out across the navigation station, calculating our course headings with a divider compass and a parallel ruler. "Dead reckoning" was what he called this process for determining the boat's position by estimating the direction and distance we had traveled.

My job was to steer by the compass, to keep the boat on the calculated course heading. But had I stayed on course? Were his calculations accurate? As we finally neared the coast of Michigan, fireworks lit the darkening skies as harbor communities celebrated the Fourth of July. We knew a safe harbor was within reach. We just weren't sure which one.

Before the next crossing, we installed Loran, a long-range navigation system that determines boat position based on signals received from radio transmitters. Rubin's job got easier. Mine did not. Only when we added "James," my name for the autopilot designed to keep the boat on a set course, was I finally able to focus on something other than the large black ball of the compass.

"Home, James," I cried with delight the first time I relaxed in the cockpit and watched James crank the wheel to adjust for fluctuations in wind and waves. We even played gin rummy one flat, light air crossing. I must have won the penny-a-point pot because after that trip, Rubin insisted we turn on the motor and "motor sail" whenever boat speed dropped below six knots. No more cockpit rummy.

"Rubin, the GPS says it is only six feet up there," I say, alarm increasing the closer we inch toward the small, boulder-lined waterway. "It shows giant rocks submerged on all sides. If we get in trouble, I have no space to turn around."

"The iPad says we can make it. It says eight feet."

He swings down to the cabin to look again at the charts.

"The charts say we're good," he hollers.

Preprinted charts are the least accurate source for depth. Printed the prior year, they cannot accurately capture the effects of winter's sparse ice coverage, few heavy spring rains, and the unseasonably hot summer temperatures. This year, lake levels are at near record lows.

The engine speed lever is as low as it will go, and yet the narrow channel is fast approaching. It must be the current, I think, and anxiety releases a river of adrenaline racing through my body.

"The iPad is probably the most accurate." He's back in the cockpit, rechecking the screen.

"But isn't this a new GPS chip?" I counter, sliding the engine into neutral.

When I first met Rubin, he was what marketers consider an "early adopter." Before I was involved in purchase decisions, he bought the first microwave on the market, one of the few models manufactured with turn dials; an eight-track cassette player; a Beta VCR, quickly outdated by VHS; a CB radio, obsolete with the introduction of cell phones. I typically wait for the kinks to get worked out, the prices to drop, and the market to accept the technology before I make the plunge. Since we've been married, major technology purchases are always spirited negotiations. The iPad with a navigation application is new technology. I don't trust it.

The current continues to propel the boat forward. The depth indicator says we are now down to eight feet. The water is so clear I can see every crack in every boulder beneath the surface.

"Rubin, what do you want to do?" There is an edge of panic in my voice. I know what he wants to do. He wants to go for it, shave the extra two hours off a long day. He's ready to tie up for the night, kick back, and have a cocktail.

"I think we can make it." He comes back to look at the GPS screen in front of me, the looming black numbers that say we cannot. He looks at my face.

"Okay," he sighs. "Go ahead and turn around."

"Thank you," I whisper.

The older I get, the more simplicity appeals to me. And while Loran is no longer available, and I would never give up James, has all this technology made sailing better? Easier? More fun? I know how I'd answer that question this afternoon. Rubin, back huddled over his iPad, would no doubt have a different response. After all these years together, it keeps our negotiations lively.

PUSH-BUTTON BOATING

Hanging on to the wheel, I stretch my body out to the side of the sailboat, straining to get a view of my husband in the bow. His floppy sunhat hides his head. Legs dangle over the edge as he hunches forward, slowly pulling on the first of two anchor lines. Despite the distance between us, I can see his shoulder muscles tightening, his arms flexing with each tug at the line.

I look up at the wind indicator on the top of the mast to make sure I'm pointed into the wind. For a quick second, I push the throttle forward, hoping to relieve some of the pressure, to make it easier for him to pull up the chain and Bruce anchor embedded in the sand. And then I switch back to neutral, cringing as I see the strain surging through his upper body.

I watch the first of 140 feet of wet line drop into the anchor locker, waiting for the clanking of chain, longing for any hint this ordeal is nearing its end. First, Rubin retrieves the thirty-three-pound Bruce anchor, a round, plow-like anchor ideal for rocks and mud. Then he hauls up the twenty-one-pound Fortress, a high-end Danforth anchor that looks as if its two giant teeth will cut permanently into the sandy soil. We drop both each night, a safety measure to prevent the boat from coming loose, drifting into another boat, rolling up on shore, or silently floating out to sea. Despite the anchors, neither of us sleeps well.

I know this trip is for me. And I love him for that. And while his good-natured, easy-going smile makes it easy to forget the strain on his aging body, upending the anchors is a reminder. Our boat is truly not equipped for wilderness trips. If we are going to continue taking long cruises that include the quiet stillness of rocking in a remote bay under the flickering lights of the stars, we need a different boat.

"But I love our boat," a side of me whispers.

My mind counters.

Newer boats have an anchor windlass system on the foredeck with a button to push to electronically raise and lower the anchor. Many have a generator humming to power the electronic necessities, often including heat and air-conditioning. They have roller-furling sails that make it easier, safer to reef during storms—sails controlled by a power winch and a button, rather than by muscles cranking a stainless-steel winch. Our 1987 Hunter is Spartan by comparison. Its design thwarts most efforts to upgrade to the newer electronic conveniences. It was built for diehard sailors like us.

Until we began aging.

Many of our sailing buddies have already transitioned to small daysailers, trawlers, even powerboats. Rubin, who loves any excuse to look at boats, is already investigating options. He points out boats he wants me to consider, suggests I take photographs of his favorites. He talks about attending the Miami and Annapolis boat shows and chartering a trawler over the winter to "check it out."

But I'm not ready. I've become attached. I know every inch of this boat, lived on it for three years, sailed it for more than fifteen. We purchased it to provide "balance" to my lopsided life dominated by career. Behind her helm, I've learned confidence, humility, humor, and love for the great waters that keep me afloat during times of darkness.

To abandon this boat for the modern conveniences of a newer model feels wrong. Until I watch the man I love struggling to pull up anchors. Then I am not so sure.

THUMBPRINT OF LIGHT

*A*s a teenager, I dreamed of canoeing the Boundary Waters of Canada, of immersing myself into a wilderness so raw, so untouched, as to challenge the very essence of my existence.

Now, decades later, I am sitting in the cockpit of our forty-foot sailboat, surrounded by remote, uninhabited islands lining the passage from Georgian Bay to Lakes Superior, Huron, and Michigan, while I eye the loons. Beneath me, the boat rocks gently, responding to a current tugging at the anchor line. It is not a river. It is not a canoe. It is not even a negotiated vacation. It is a gift from my husband's heart to nourish and replenish mine.

This journey into the North Channel, which began weeks ago as we sailed through the Lake Macatawa channel into the southeastern corner of Lake Michigan and up a coast I call home, then under the inspiring Mackinac Bridge and across Lake Huron, through the North Channel and finally into Georgian Bay, has surpassed even my greatest longings of youth.

The wilderness is all me. The sailboat is all Rubin. And me.

Through the lens of my camera, I see the defining white stripes on the necks of the two loons before they plunge into the glassy waters of the North Channel. I wait patiently for them to resurface, while scanning waters yet to be touched by the tiny diamonds of early sunlight or the ripples of the day's wind. The tweeting song of redwing blackbirds perched among the dusted tips of the nearby cattails floats across the cove in which we are anchored. As the stillness of night transitions to dawn, I silently ask a familiar question.

How do I reflect the thumbprint of light placed on my soul at birth?

I am learning it is not what I *do* in life that matters. It is how I choose to *live* that life that defines me. When I pause and notice even the tiniest things—like the feathery white wings of the Olympia Marble butterfly, striped with the lime-green color of spring, or the powder-blue pinstripe markings on the White Admiral butterfly—a sort of calmness settles about me. I feel connected, as if God has showered me everywhere with beacons of light, thumbprints, to remind me I am not alone. And at that moment, I feel such gratitude, such joy surging through my heart, I feel as if intuitively I have found my answer.

Loons mate for life and are inseparable. I see the pair I've been watching surface further out toward the open waters of the channel. In the main cabin below, I hear dishes clanging and know the blondish-gray, curly-haired head of my mate will soon appear through the companionway. His wide smile cuts through the white scruffy beard of vacation. In his hands will be two large mugs of coffee. And while my face is weathered by the sun and wrinkled with age, I know, even before hearing his voice, the way our day will begin. For while the wind may switch directions, the lake may build from serene stillness to ridges of frothing fury, my every day begins with the same three words from the captain, boataholic, and man I married.

"Good morning, beautiful."

It gives him a negotiating advantage from the get-go.

PROTECTING OUR HOME: 2012–2016

*Boats do not sail without effort. The same is true for dreams . . .
particularly those dreams that touch not just our own weathered
hands, but the soft, smooth hands of our children.*

This is our home. And home is worth protecting.

"WHAT IS YOUR DEEPEST DREAM?"

The question on the page stops me, and I place the book on my lap, reflecting on a prayer whispered earlier as dawn etched the clouds hovering over the jagged peaks of the Santa Catalina Mountains of Arizona. The question, posed to author BettyClare Moffatt in her book, *Soulwork: Clearing the Mind, Opening the Heart, Replenishing the Spirit*,[8] startled her, as it does me.

What is my innermost dream?

Thanksgiving will mark two years since I received a phone call that determined where and how I spent my time for the next twenty-four months; how I shaped my priorities and defined my purpose in life. This month, for the first time, the long list of to-dos associated with the medical decisions regarding my dad's care and the financial and legal challenges associated with his passing will disappear. Despite the heartbreaking pain associated with his decline, the overwhelming sense of responsibility for making decisions for him while caring for my mother, I would not trade these years for any in my lifetime. For while the emotional anguish often seemed unbearable, the experience taught me that no desperate plea whispered over the dry, powdery sand of the desert goes unanswered. Ever.

I stood this morning as sunrise brushed the wispy leaves of the mesquite trees, the chalky gray stalks of the teddy bear chollas, the array of olive and milky-green cactuses defining my favorite prickly wash. "Now what?" I prayed. For my mother, whom I am visiting in Arizona, is strong, healthy again. My father is gone. My focus needs to shift. But where? What am I meant to do? I wander the deepest, blackest caverns of my mind. Lost. Chasing the same questions I asked when I left corporate life eight years ago, second-guessing my earlier answers. I am floundering in a self-imposed muddle of misery.

Staring at the rocky crest of mountains defining the eastern horizon, I asked the angels to nudge me in the right direction, to open a door wide enough to shine a beam of light on the path I am meant to follow, to help me figure out my life. But no revelation rolled through me, just the quiet peace of dawn dissolving into day. I turned and continued to jog the silent streets of my mother's community.

The book now on my lap is tattered and frayed from use, for it is a favorite companion during times of uncertainty, periods of transition. Like now. And while I have read it numerous times, it always inspires.

"What is your deepest dream?" a friend and spiritual mentor asked the author. BettyClare Moffatt, like me, waffled in self-doubt, saw challenges too daunting to overcome, distressed over things of which she had no control. But her friend was relentless, repeating the question until finally the truth flowed freely.

"My deepest dream," I read, "is to write wise and loving books that touch the hearts of women everywhere. That make a difference in the world. That serve in some way. That are good, true, and beautiful."

I gasp! This is my dream! My heart-felt desire! Placed on hold but still flickering like the bluish-gold flame of a pilot light.

"But can I do it? . . . Can I really do it?" Moffatt asks.

"I have no doubt," replies her friend. And from that conversation, the sacred book I now hold was created, published, distributed throughout the world.

A nudge. A sliver of light shining through a crack in the darkness.

But can I? Doubts swirl like the blinding dust of a windstorm sweeping across the desert floor. Can my words make a difference? Can I compose lyrical sentences, paragraphs, stories that touch the hearts of others? Do I have the toughness to handle criticism? The perseverance to make writing a priority? Can I create my deepest dream?

"I have no doubt," I say softly to the roadrunner flitting across the rocky terrain behind the prickly pear cactus. "I have no doubt," I call to the family of quails scurrying away. "I have no doubt," I holler to the puffy clouds floating across the ragged edges of the mountains.

But the queasiness inside my stomach says otherwise. And I know it is time to return home, to return to the lake that defines me.

EMERGING FROM THE COCOON

*L*ooking out at an auditorium filled with people roughly my age, I admit to feeling naked.

"For the first time, I am giving a talk without my photography," I explain. "Technology has leapfrogged the Visitor Center here at the P.J. Hoffmaster State Park. The twenty-year-old projector won't handle high-definition photographs. And while in the past I've brought my own projector, with Apple's new operating system I now need 'an interpreter' for my computer and my projector to work together. And that little black box requires a wireless system, something not available here at the park." [9]

It is as if God is sending me a wake-up call.

Photography has become as important to me as words. It connects me with nature, with the present moment. It brings me joy to share it with others. But what is becoming increasingly apparent is that, to honor that artistic voice of my right brain—my photographs—I need that left brain of mine to tackle the unfamiliar language of new technology.

"How many people own cell phones?" I ask the audience. All but three of the roughly sixty people raise their hands. I'm one of the three.

"How many people own eBook readers?" I continue. The majority raises their hands. I, too, own an eBook reader. But I admit to the group that I still prefer picking up books at the local bookstore.

"I have what I call my sacred bookshelves. On them are authors I hold in great esteem, whose words inspire me and weave threads of influence into my own tapestry of writing. The bookshelves are built into a magical wall. If I tug on the center shelf, the wall of books opens slowly, revealing a secret passageway into my clothes closet. On one side of the wall is a world of words and dreams. On the other is the reality of living."

Curious, I ask questions of the people listening to my talk, and they confirm my hunch. Almost all watch YouTube videos and/or make them; participate regularly on social media; check websites or blogs to learn about items of interest. And while almost all had read a book in the last twelve months, not everyone raises a hand.

If I am going to be an effective storyteller, sharing my passion for protecting the Great Lakes to influence the political will of others, I must embrace the new technology. I need a website, a blog, a Facebook page.

The thought of entering the vast, unknown world of cyberspace is terrifying. I am a private person who spent most of her adult life behind the veil of political anonymity. And yet, my sacred bookshelves are filled with authors who have been willing to peel back the crusted layers of life to reveal their own imperfect selves, their messy, sometimes bloody journeys to find their truth and speak it clearly, bravely, publicly.

It is time I do the same.

At first, the thought of using my photographs to create an inspiring and thought-provoking website arouses the artistic thread running through me. However, the realities of muddling through complicated website programs designed for people trained in computer languages almost derails me. Why does technology have to be so difficult?

About the time I am spiraling into despair, a friend's son, Michael Sturrus, points me to an intuitive platform for creating websites. Like a patient art instructor, he shows me how to design my own pages, how to embed photographs and text, how to link to other sites, create a blog page, paint with different fonts and colors.

It is thrilling.

With my confidence bolstered, I plunge into the technology and post my first blog. Titled, "Learning Faith," it includes a slide show of butterflies with the following reflection:

> *Life's transitions remind me of a caterpillar dangling in a cocoon of darkness. It takes faith to believe one can emerge and spread one's wings in a flurry of color before finally soaring above all doubts, all fears, all heartache.*

I am emerging from my cocoon.

MY READER

Sitting on our front porch, feet curled up on the edge of the chair, knees scrunched against my chest, I am rocking. I can feel the cool breeze off Lake Michigan, hear the wind rustling the dense canopy of leaves overhead, see a few tiny wildflowers peeking through the edges of the forest.

Nestled in a pocket of pachysandra growing between the rock wall of our porch and the wooden boardwalk cantilevering over the dune of our front yard, sits my reader. She is a young woman, in her late twenties. She, too, sits with knees near her chest as she balances a book in one hand, a glass of wine in the other. She appears to be listening, intently. But her face shows no emotion. The book speaks of intellectual curiosity. The wine tells me she takes neither me, nor herself, too seriously.

A sculpture of rusted steel, she was a gift from my mother, selected by my husband to share the floating platform which is home to two giant anchors shipped from somewhere on the east coast.

The anchors are all Rubin. The reader is all me.

What would I tell her, my reader, if she were my daughter? Can I explain why the eastern shores of Lake Michigan touch my heart like no other place? Can I counter all the negative press? All the reasons young people her age are fleeing this region? Why voices of cynicism and despair are always the loudest? And how difficult it is to learn to listen and speak one's truth?

I keep rocking.

I have no pearls of wisdom. Only eight tumultuous years of experience.

But I want her to know that, after sailing this massive body of fresh water, after hiking the mountains of dunes and miles of sandy beaches, and bicycling along the forests, rivers, and marshes stretching from the Indiana Dunes to Mackinac Island, I consider this part of the world a sacred place. And I, like many others, am committed to protecting it for her and her children.

I want her to have hope.

In my former life, I remember jogging past the White House on my frequent business trips to the nation's capital. I ran through the World War II, Viet Nam, and Korean War Memorials, up the steps of the Lincoln Memorial, along the Tidal Basin to the Franklin D. Roosevelt and Jefferson Memorials, and past the Washington Monument. Humbled by the wisdom of our past leaders and the dedication and sacrifices made by the men and women in our military, I was honored to be running among their shadows. I remember turning east and running alongside the Smithsonian, barely noticing the unique architecture of its many museums. My eyes were on the Capitol, etched by the glowing light of early morning.

Within its domed walls, those we choose to represent us shape our future. Our choice. Our country. Our duty to those who crafted our Constitution, to those men and women who have died to give us a voice in government, is to understand the issues, weigh the tradeoffs, and make our voices heard as we search to find balance in a world with so many competing priorities.

I want my reader to choose to engage.

I don't know that she will listen. But I have to try. Tapping the science and the art, the adventures and the concerns, my left brain and my right, I enter the world of social media and begin posting a monthly blog. With photographs. And because this is a book about the Great Lakes, I have included a handful of slightly modified blogs that address long-term issues too critical to ignore. While the specific details may have changed over time, sadly, the fundamental issues remain unresolved.

I want my reader to be informed, as well as engaged.

SEPTEMBER 2013 BLOG:
TERROR IN THE STRAITS

*I*t was more than two decades ago, but I remember my heart pounding beneath a raincoat crushed against my body by a stiff lifejacket zipped firmly from waist to neck. Sheets of rain engulfed me as I attempted to keep the sailboat pointed into the wind, to keep gale-force winds from grabbing the giant mainsail and whipping the boat into nearby shallow waters, riddled with rocks and giant boulders. The sail flapped angrily overhead, the fabric whipping through the air and the cracking sound shattering any sense of inner confidence.

"Whatever you do, keep the boat in the channel," Rubin hollered before dashing out of the cockpit and disappearing into the wall of sleeting rain. He raced to the mast to reef the sail, to reduce its size and regain control. Giant haystacks of water danced wildly alongside, their white frothy tops confirming the storm's madness. The wind pelted my face with stinging rain, blinding me to Rubin's progress, preventing me from seeing even an outline of a channel marker. I had never been in the Straits of Mackinac; never sailed through Grays Reef, a twenty-two-square-mile stretch of north-eastern Lake Michigan defined by jagged, rocky ledges just below the surface of the water.

After looking briefly at the charts, I was sure the passage was the width of a river, too narrow to spin the boat should Rubin be flung overboard. Mentally, I practiced the drill and saw myself tossing the lifebuoy, yanking the halyard to drop the sail, and spinning the wheel to backtrack and find Rubin, to pull him from the icy waters of Lake Michigan. A stream of prayers accompanied a vision of the boat smashing into the rocks, the splintering of fiberglass, and the freezing water rushing over my body as the current dragged me toward the Mackinac Bridge.

It used to be that if one were to ask me to define terror, I would recount that first passage through Grays Reef.

Until now, autumn of 2013. Until seeing a video that shows that underneath this stretch of often treacherous waters lie two pipelines, sixty years old and carrying twenty million gallons of crude oil each day.

Until hearing Dr. Val Klump, Professor and Associate Dean of Research at the University of Wisconsin-Milwaukee School of Freshwater Sciences, caution that the science used to clean up and minimize oil-spill damage in the ocean most likely will not apply in the freshwaters of the Great Lakes.

Until reading a report by Jeff Alexander and Beth Wallace, titled "Sunken Hazard," and learning the owner of the pipelines is Canadian-based Enbridge Energy, the same company whose line ruptured in 2010 and dumped one million gallons of diluted tar sands oil into the Kalamazoo River. Roughly 175 thousand gallons still blacken the riverbed years later, the heavy globs of tar-like product nearly impossible to remove without severely damaging the river's ecosystem.

Until learning from the "Sunken Hazard" report found on the National Wildlife Federation website[10] that the oil pipeline through the Straits is the gateway to an underground network of pipes running across Michigan and out to cities throughout the U.S. and eastern Canada. According to the report, Enbridge's environmental track record is abysmal and includes 800 spills in North America between 1999 and 2010. The company has a history of investing in reactionary responses, rather than in preventive methods like replacing outdated pipelines or improving monitoring practices. Government agencies have repeatedly warned and fined the company, even pointing to its failure to maintain the pipeline as the cause of the Kalamazoo River disaster. Despite the difficulty of removing the diluted tar sands oil from the river, Enbridge plans to increase the amount of oil flowing through the Straits by almost two million gallons per day. Not diluted tar sands oil, fortunately—at least for the moment, but oil, just the same.

I have a new definition of terror.

For while my legs have trembled with fear in subsequent passages through the Straits when unexpected high winds knocked our boat on its side or gray fog blanketed a freighter off our stern, I have also tasted dawn in the shadows of the Mackinac Bridge. I have watched the sun's diamonds dance in our wake, breathed the crisp dampness of early morning's air, felt the boat gliding through little wrinkles created as the wind skipped merrily across the lake's surface. I have listened to the delighted calls of shorebirds celebrating day's beginning.

Terror is envisioning the sparkling blue waters of Lake Michigan and Lake Huron covered with the slimy sheen of oil. It is knowing that there is a possibility the same thick, gloppy oil product poisoning the Kalamazoo riverbed, just south of our house, could also blacken the sandy floor of the Straits. It is knowing that science cannot repair the damage, that prevention is the only alternative.

I have been told the future of the Great Lakes depends on good science and political will. We do not have the science to contain a spill. We must depend on the efforts of people with purpose and passion. That means signing petitions, sending e-mails to elected representatives, talking about it with others. [11]

For me, it also means researching and writing stories, posting them on my blog. But writing is one thing. Expanding the reach of my blog is something completely different. Online publishing—or any publishing—is an industry in which I have little knowledge and no relationships. At times, it feels impossible.

JULY 2014 BLOG:
COLD KNOWS NO PRIDE

Lake Michigan Crossing
July 16, 2014
Frankfort to Sturgeon Bay
Wind in the face
Mid-lake water
temperature 33.6 degrees.
No sun.
No flies.
No fog.
No fingers.
Frozen
but safe.

A good day.[12]

AUGUST 2014 BLOG:
GOOD SCIENCE AND THE
POLITICAL WILL

*T*he newspaper headline is jarring: "400,000 Toledo Residents Without Drinking Water." The story grabs the attention of the national media in the summer of 2014, a summer riddled with crises of seemingly unparalleled proportions. I am tempted to bury my head in a good novel, to plunk my feet in the sand and enjoy the summer breeze tiptoeing across Lake Michigan, for I am weary of crises. But the plight facing Ohio residents affects me, too.

It was less than a year ago, in September of 2013, that I watched a man approach the microphone in a jam-packed public hearing of the International Joint Commission (IJC). He was holding a jar of what looked like grungy split pea soup.

"This is the water that came out of my faucet last week, just before the city shut down the water treatment plant," the resident of Carroll Township, Ohio, told a crowd of several hundred people, including Rubin and me.

Carroll Township is thirty-eight miles west of Sandusky Bay, the body of water in which we once kept our boat when careers transferred us from Chicago to Columbus, Ohio, in 1990. I remember peering over the lifeline of *The Inevitable* on its maiden voyage into Lake Erie.

"I can see the ridges of sand on the bottom of the lake!" I exclaimed joyfully. "It is so clear! So clean!"

And it was. The U.S. and Canadian Great Lakes Water Quality Agreement and the U.S. Clean Water Act, both passed in 1972, brought the shallow lake back to life from the days when the Cuyahoga River caught fire in Cleveland, when algal sludge marred the lake's surface, when the smell and taste of the lake were as foul as Easter eggs rotting in forgotten hiding places.

Lake Erie was considered a success story. Until now.

On one hand, the Carroll Township community was fortunate that the water-treatment supervisor noticed the potentially lethal toxin originating from Lake Erie's blue-green algae, we were told at the hearing. Monitoring for this toxin is not required by the Environmental Protection Agency, and acceptable levels of toxicity have yet to be established. On the other hand, it was heartbreaking to hear the quality of Lake Erie water had deteriorated so dramatically, so quickly.

According to the IJC, an organization created by the Canadian and U.S. governments under the Boundary Waters Treaty of 1909, Lake Erie became a top priority when the worst algal blooms in the lake's history were recorded in 2011. Warmer temperatures, the filtering of the water by invasive zebra and quagga mussels, the shallow depth of the lake, and the excessive levels of phosphorus from agricultural and urban runoff had created an algal bloom that was threatening the water quality of Lake Erie, speakers explained to the crowd. Transitioning the lake back to the clear, clean water of the 1990s hinged on federal, state, and local intervention, particularly the states of Michigan, Ohio, Indiana, New York, Pennsylvania, and the province of Ontario. And it would require the commitment and involvement of the people of the Lake Erie watershed.

The sobering assessment and list of sixteen recommendations were outlined in a report released in February of 2014, titled, "A Balanced Diet for Lake Erie: Reducing Phosphorus Loadings and Harmful Algal Blooms."

"The future of the lakes hinges on good science and political will," Lana Pollack, U.S. chair of the IJC, told us at the meeting. "The science is clear. What is needed is the political will."

But while science provides crisp, black-and-white answers, I am finding most solutions are negotiated steps among shades of gray. Political will is not easy work. It requires the leadership of people who can build bridges among a diverse group of stakeholders—not walls that divide and polarize.

In a global environment, how do farms compete while adopting practices known to protect nearby water supplies when competitors do not? How can families afford to put responsibly produced meat, chicken, and produce on tables when money is tight? How do struggling communities pay for green infrastructure to minimize the effects of miles of roads and acres of parking lots? How do they finance the replacement of antiquated sewage treatment facilities and address aging, leaky septic systems?

Because our sources of water—streams, rivers, and lakes—cut across county, state, and country boundaries, there is a level of complexity added to an already emotionally and politically charged environment. Tackling agricultural and industrial runoff may not be popular, but it is essential.

Ask the man from Carroll Township. Ask the parents with small children living in Toledo.

The challenges we face today, balancing economic prosperity with the protection of limited natural resources, are not new. What has changed is the scarcity of clean, fresh water on the planet, the urgency in the need to reverse the ecological slide of the existing resources, and the increasing price tag associated with delay.

Sometimes it takes a crisis to spark political will. Is Toledo, a medium-sized city of less than a million people, enough of a spark? Will anything change?

"We are responsible for our efforts, not the results." I remember Alene Moris's counsel.

Closing my eyes, I see again the little girl on the cover of a book of poetry, enchanted by all the wondrous gifts of nature, creating a world of endless possibilities.

What she needs now is faith.

JUNE 2015 BLOG:
VOICE OF A FISHERMAN'S DAUGHTER

Where is that woman who squared her shoulders, took a deep breath, and stepped into the Detroit Tiger dugout as the first woman sports editor to interview legendary baseball manager Billy Martin?

Where is that employee with the spunk to negotiate an opportunity to play Augusta National Golf Course? Who, given the chance, invited two other women to accompany her? "First time in course history," according to the caddie, "three women teed off together" as part of a foursome.[13]

Where is that cocky athlete who charged the net with such fervor she earned a spot on the 1973 Michigan State University Varsity Tennis Team, winners of the Big 10 championship?

Where is that brazenly confident person who slipped through customs in the South Africa airport with only two hundred dollars in her wallet, sure she could find a job to support her stay in the country?

I know she's there, buried under a heaping sand dune of humbling experiences and subsequent self-reflection that seems to mellow her with age . . .

Until I hear from a leading scientist in the region that Aquatic Invasive Species (AIS) remain the greatest threat to the Great Lakes waterways. It tops the list of threats, including sewage contamination, habitat destruction, toxic pollution, climate change, and polluted runoff.

According to the National Oceanic and Atmospheric Administration, more than 180 nonindigenous species have been reported in the Great Lakes basin. The first known to arrive in the Great Lakes was the sea lamprey, first sighted in the 1830s. Almost two hundred years later, the sea lamprey still ravages our waterways, sucking the life out of native fish.

Why does it matter?

In 2012, The Nature Conservancy commissioned Anderson Economic Group to find the answer. The report points to the impact AIS have on water-treatment facilities, power generation, industrial facilities using surface water, tourism, government agencies, the fishing industry, and even everyday consumers. The effects are sobering. According to the report, AIS cost the region more than $100 million annually.

But it is the effect they have on our fishing populations that stirs the spirited underpinnings of my youth.

Lake trout, sturgeon, and lake herring, while making a comeback, are a fraction of what they were in the mid-1900s. Blue pike and Lake Ontario Atlantic salmon are considered virtually extinct. According to the Nature Conservancy report, fish catches that once measured 147 million pounds per year in the late 1800s now weigh only 110 million pounds. And while the catches should have increased because of population growth and improved technology, the decrease is attributed to a combination of "over-fishing, declining food at key points on the food chain, and the presence of AIS."[14]

While the science is clear and the economics compelling, it is something else that tugs at the bold, fearless thread of my youth, urging me to claw my way out of the dune of introspection and get involved. It is the memory of a father and a daughter standing alongside a river, casting and mending our lines. It is the picture of us silently waiting, watching for that quick sliver of a fish to dart through the shadows toward our flies. Even now, years after his death, I can feel the deep, intimate connection I had with this man who found peace holding a rod and reel.

It is a memory that should not be denied any daughter of a fisherman. Ever.

Currently before Congress, the bipartisan "Defending Our Great Lakes Act of 2015" gives federal agencies the authority to take immediate action to stop the spread of Asian Carp and other invasive species between the Great Lakes and Mississippi River basins. Passage depends on our collective willingness to contact federal representatives and make this legislation a priority.

Squaring my shoulders and taking a deep breath, I dust off the sand and add my voice to those insisting, "We can do better. We must do better." And once again, I am that woman who believes anything is possible.

NOVEMBER 2015 BLOG:
THE SEARCH FOR BALANCE ON
THE INDIANA SHORE

She is Lee Botts, a woman in her mid-eighties with eyes that sparkle when she speaks of the coast of northern Indiana, who reminds me passion and collaboration are two sides of the same coin.

I had not met Lee when I took my first step on a path winding through a marsh reflecting the browns and grays of life, teetering between the blistering winds of winter and the frosty air of early April. The year was 2008, and I was giddy with excitement at surviving my first night camping alone in a tent on a campsite in the Indiana Dunes National Lakeshore. My icy fingers balled into fists and stuffed inside the warm pockets of a sweatshirt, I stood on the boardwalk overlooking the marsh and listened to the chattering of birds that perched on branches touched by the first blushes of spring.

I thought my heart would burst with joy at the intimacy I felt with nature, to all hints of life stretching before me.

That first hike on my trek up the eastern coast of Lake Michigan was made in ecological ignorance. I did not realize there were different types of sand dunes, each formed by the powerful forces of wind, water, and the glaciers of the past. The Indiana Dunes are considered linear dunes, formed from the irregular cycles of high and low water levels. As I began hiking into the forested mountains of sand, the seeds of passion began sprouting with each step, each new sighting of spring. And passion, for me, was synonymous with protecting.

I suspect the same was true for Henry Chandler Cowles, a botanist from the University of Chicago. Publishing an article in 1886, titled "Ecological Relations of the Vegetation on Sand Dunes of Lake Michigan," Cowles established himself as the "father of plant ecology." His research sparked a battle to protect the Indiana Dunes from development, from the removal of sand for manufacturing, from the industrialization that was occurring forty miles to the west. For while Cowles was bringing attention to the biodiversity of the dunes, John D. Rockefeller and Elbert Gary were building the infrastructures of oil refineries and steel mills, respectively, on the southwestern corner of Lake Michigan. Shunned by Chicago's city fathers, who wanted to keep the waterfront free from manufacturing, Rockefeller and Gary located their facilities in northern Indiana, creating thousands of jobs while providing kerosene, gas, and steel to the rapidly growing city of Chicago.

I can remember standing at the end of that April day on top of Mount Tom, a dune towering almost 200 feet high in the

Indiana Dunes State Park. Filling my lungs with the cool breeze off the lake, I turned my gaze west, hoping to see the first splashes of sunset. Instead, I saw the smokestacks of Gary, Indiana, and a sad outrage replaced my bliss.

Decisions made more than one hundred years ago had shaped my view of the landscape in all directions. I turned my back on northwest Indiana.

What I did not know then but recognize now is that under the leadership of Lee Botts, because of her determination and passion, the water and air quality of northwestern Indiana has improved by almost ninety percent since 1990. By founding organizations like the Lake Michigan Federation (now expanded to all five lakes and known as the Alliance for the Great Lakes), the Indiana Dunes Learning Center, and the Northwest Indiana Quality of Life Council, Lee has found ways to create dialogue among diverse stakeholders, to broker paths through the minefields of polarity, to create a shared vision, and then find collaborative solutions to make it happen.

One of the top priorities of this coalition of federal, state, and local organizations, business and union leaders, scientists, environmental groups, and private residents is restoring the Grand Calumet River. Pooling resources, they are cleaning up a river listed as one of the forty-three most toxic waterways in the 1987 Great Lakes Water Quality Agreement between the United States and Canada. The goal is to complete all requirements outlined in the agreement by 2019, so the river can be delisted.

This sounds nothing short of miraculous. But it is not a miracle. It is hard, expensive work.

According to the agreement, delisting requires the removal of all Beneficial Use Impairments (BUI), "changes in the chemical, physical, or biological integrity of the Great Lakes system that are significant enough to cause impairment to designated users." [15]

It sounds complicated, but the fourteen impairments used to measure the quality of the water are fairly straightforward. The list includes: any restrictions on fish and wildlife consumption; tainting of fish and wildlife flavor; degradation of fish and wildlife populations; discovering fish tumors or other deformities; detection of bird or animal deformities or other reproduction problems; degradation of the flora and fauna found on the lake or river bottom; restrictions on dredging; the presence of undesirable algae or pollution caused by chemical nutrients such as phosphorus; restrictions on drinking-water; beach closings; degradation of aesthetics; added costs to agriculture and industry; degradation of phytoplankton and zooplankton populations; and loss of fish and wildlife habitat.

The Grand Calumet River had more BUIs than any other waterway on the Great Lakes.

Rather than turning my back on northwest Indiana, I want to learn more. Gary, Indiana, is an example of what can happen when a diverse people in a seemingly impossible situation decide to collaborate and choose to blend passion with purpose, so they can leave a clean, healthy, and economically vibrant place for future generations to call home. It is democracy at its best. [16]

DECEMBER 2015 BLOG:
THE ASIAN CARP CONUNDRUM

I am drawn to the snippets of color on the beach like a hummingbird flitting about a summer's garden. Balloon ribbons. Straws. Shotgun wads—pieces of white plastic that look like bottle caps with four open fingers—discharged when people shoot skeet. Plastic water bottles. Empty bait containers. Cigarette butts. In my quest to return the shore to its natural state, I zigzag across the sand, stuffing each piece of junk into a trash bag.

The litter tells a story . . . and not a good one.

There are times I do not see the sparkle of sunlight on the pooling water or notice the patterns drawn in the wet sand by a recoiling wave.

Balance has never been my strong suit.

I think about a hand clutching a jar of the greenish soup from Lake Erie; the photograph of trucks hauling away Wisconsin's pristine sand for use in fracking; the video of the sixty-year-old oil pipeline lying untethered on the sandy floor of Lake Michigan one mile west of the Mackinac Bridge. I feel the unseasonably warm December temperatures and know Lake Superior will not receive the level of ice cover needed to keep our fresh water from evaporating, to keep our water levels high enough for commercial and recreational boaters to pass through our harbors.

On and on I go ... worrying.

And so, I now take a camera with me on my walks alongside Lake Michigan ... and the bag for trash. I need both. Facts and passion. Reality and hope.

I do not cover much ground quickly.

This morning's walk is slower than most. I am deeply troubled by the recurring question: can we keep the invasive Asian carp out of Lake Michigan?

While the leading edge of the adult carp population has remained the same since 2006, in late October of 2015, the juvenile carp—measuring between five and seven inches, were found sixty-six miles closer to Lake Michigan than reported earlier in the year. According to the U.S. Fish and Wildlife Service, it appears the juvenile fish become trapped in the underwater spaces between commercial barges and are then inadvertently transported across the electronic barriers designed to keep the Asian carp from reaching Lake Michigan.

No one wants these prolific species of silver, bighead, black, and grass Asian carp with voracious appetites to invade the Great Lakes. The silver and bighead are particularly troublesome. They devour the plankton populations, the bottom of the food chain that sustains other fish populations. The silver species jump wildly out of the water at the humming of an approaching motor, injuring recreational boaters. Experts say the invasion of the Asian carp could decimate the $7 billion Great Lakes fishing industry and the $16 billion recreational boating industry.

But the solution is complicated by the imperfection of the science needed to monitor and deter movement of the fish as they swim up the Mississippi and Illinois Rivers toward Lake Michigan. It's politicized by the diverse interests of those affected by possible solutions. And ultimately, the best answers could be derailed by the price tag.

Time is working against us.

Preventing the carp from reaching Lake Michigan depends on the speed of the Army Corps of Engineers in determining the feasibility of a new lock and dam system under design at the Brandon Road Lock & Dam, roughly twenty-five miles from the lake. They will not have answers until 2017, or later.

During the interim, the Asian Carp Regional Coordinating Committee is leading efforts across a multitude of agencies, organizations, and universities working diligently to outsmart the carp. Their success depends on the efficacy of the electronic barriers, water guns, harvesting efforts, carbon dioxide released at dam entrances, and an earthen berm in Indiana. It depends on their ability to use environmental DNA, electro-fishing, poison, and other techniques to monitor the movement of the fish. And it depends on the continued prioritization and funding of the efforts of the Army Corps of Engineers by Congress and the White House.

Experts agree the only sure way to prevent the two-way exchange of aquatic invasive species from flowing between the Mississippi River and Lake Michigan is to reverse the decisions made more than one hundred years ago and restore the natural divide that existed between the two basins. A study commissioned by the Great Lakes Commission and the Great Lakes and St. Lawrence Cities Initiative demonstrated that full separation, also called hydrological separation, was a feasible and viable option. It is also very controversial.

The Chicago Sanitary and Ship Canal, a 28-mile-long and 160-foot-wide artificial canal, was built at the turn of the 20th century to flush Chicago's sewage and industrial waste toward the Mississippi River rather than into Lake Michigan. The lake was, and remains, the source of the city's drinking water. When thousands died of typhoid fever in the 1890s, city leaders decided to reverse the flow of the Chicago and Calumet Rivers by creating the canal and connecting Lake Michigan to the Illinois River and, ultimately, the Mississippi. The canal also became an integral part of a complex waterway system that facilitates commercial barge traffic from Chicago to New Orleans.

In the early 1900s, no one considered the possibility that the new water highway would one day become a conduit for aquatic invasive species to threaten natural ecosystems from New Orleans to the St. Lawrence Seaway.

The decision had unintended consequences.

So, too, did the decision made in the 1970s by Arkansas biologists who introduced the Asian carp into polluted ponds and lagoons as an alternative to using chemicals to filter and clean the water.[17] Flooding, and the inadvertent release of the carp into the wild, began the carp's destructive march up the Mississippi River.

Ultimately, the recommendation for a long-term solution rests on the shoulders of thirty-two individuals representing the diverse interests of all major stakeholders. I am told this group, the Chicago Area Waterway System Advisory Committee, hopes to hammer out their differences and reach a consensus by December 2015.[18]

They must take into consideration the concerns of commercial navigation as well as that of the fishing and boating recreational industries. They must consider the effect of Lake Michigan's water quality if sewage effluent from Chicago and contaminated sediment from their harbors flow freely into the lake. And as the locks are currently used to control flooding, they must work in concert with those implementing the Tunnel and Reservoir Plan (TARP), an elaborate system of tunnels and reservoirs designed to channel excess water and sewage away from downtown Chicago. Its targeted completion date is 2029.

The Advisory Committee will make a recommendation, not a decision. Those we choose to represent us at the federal, state, and local levels of government will have the final say. And because there is no "they" in a democracy, the decision is on our shoulders.

Can we move quickly enough to keep these carp out of our lakes? [19]

JANUARY 2016 BLOG:
THE SHAME OF FLINT

I planned to start the year with a blog about gratitude, welcoming the bipartisan decision by the U.S. House and Senate in December of 2015 to fund another $300 million for the cleanup of the Great Lakes. But while vacationing in Florida this month, gratitude slid into shame as I saw the Flint water crisis splashed across national headlines.

I am a resident of Michigan, a citizen of "The Great Lakes State." And because I believe elected officials work for "We, the people," I feel responsible to the 100,000 residents of Flint whose drinking water has been tainted with excessive levels of lead for the last two years.

Three things bothered me while in Florida, and when I returned home and began researching the details, shame morphed into anger.

1) A state-appointed emergency manager made the decision to switch Flint's source for clean, safe drinking water. And yet, I remember the citizens of Michigan voting against the

governor-appointed emergency manager referendum placed on the ballot in November of 2012.

The primary concern of voters was that the law, originally enacted in 2011, gave significant power to state-appointed officials, to people neither elected by the people of a community nor accountable to them. It flew in the face of a democracy. And yet, in December of 2012, less than a month after the citizens of Michigan made their wishes known by voting against the governor-appointed emergency manager referendum, state lawmakers designed a new bill that gave financially troubled governments four options, all ultimately resulting in state oversight. Choosing one of the options was mandatory. This time, the new bill included appropriations for funding the salaries of the emergency managers. Bills with appropriations are not subject to voter referendum.

Governor Rick Snyder signed the new bill into law on December 27, 2012, less than sixty days after voters defeated the original bill.

2) I remember, as a young woman, standing under a scorching sun in Africa. I was penniless at the time, jobless, and desperate for a drink of water. My only recourse was to steal the water I needed to survive. No one in this country, or any country, should be in that position.

Under Roman law, more than 2,000 years ago, water was established as a common resource owned and shared by the public. The responsibility of governments was to ensure the people have access to "the air, the running water, the sea, and shores of the sea." Now called the Public Trust Doctrine, the concept was reinforced under the Magna Carta in 1215. Shared resources, like our water, were to be preserved in perpetuity for the use and enjoyment of the public.

And governments, like private trustees, were accountable to their beneficiaries in managing and protecting public trust properties. It is a concept adopted worldwide, a fundamental principle on which our democracy is based.

Michigan's government, my government, violated that principle. And for that, all involved should be held accountable—investigated and judged by the laws of this land.

3) When I see truckloads of bottled water shipped anywhere, I cringe. *National Geographic for Kids* reports that for every six water bottles used, only one makes it to the recycling bin. The rest are either sent to landfills—where it takes an average of 450 years for the plastic to decompose—or dumped as trash, littering our streets, land, and water. Certainly, I find plastic bottles when walking Lake Michigan's shores. Not as many as the balloon ribbons that fill my bag, but still plenty.

Former Flint resident and film producer Michael Moore made a public plea for people to quit sending bottled water to Flint. It's a short-term fix, he says. We would have to send 200 bottles per person per day to meet the average water needs. That equates to 20.4 million 16-oz. bottles of water per day for the next one to two years until the pipes are repaired and/or replaced. A better solution, he suggests, is to deliver two 55-gallon drums to every home in Flint. The drums can be refilled with Lake Huron water filtered safely by Detroit and delivered by trucks to Flint residents.

Logistically, it is a much smarter solution. But there are other reasons I like his idea. Bottling water, the world's scarcest resource, is the first step in the privatization of water for profit. And that is wrong. Secondly, while the Great Lakes governors and two premiers from Canada created the 2008 Compact to protect Great Lakes waters from diversions outside the region, water shipped in containers less than 5.7 gallons is not included in the agreement. It's a loophole. In other words, companies and governments cannot build pipelines or fill freighters to drain the Great Lakes without agreement from all ten government entities, but they can build water-bottling plants. The more bottled water is splashed across the news as the "safe" drinking water, the more those with the financial means will resort to drinking bottled water.

And the bottled water most likely will come from the Great Lakes region, profiting companies, not the people.

Flint teaches us that we cannot assume our elected officials will automatically prioritize clean, safe water. The monies flowing into the Great Lakes Restoration Initiative for the last five years happened because people and organizations in this region chose to make our water a priority for federal representatives; chose to create a voice so loud, so powerful, it could not be ignored. We can, we must, do the same at the local level, one community at a time.

I live in a democracy, and for that, I am very grateful. Sometimes it takes a crisis to remind me that a democracy is only as good as people are informed and involved. In this Great Lakes region, where we are blessed to live adjacent to the world's largest body of fresh surface water, it is a disgrace that the two cities in the last two years, Toledo and Flint, have not had access to clean, safe drinking water. My vote will go to those who choose to make fresh water a top priority! [20]

FEBRUARY 2016 BLOG:
THE WATER WARS HAVE BEGUN

*F*lorida has sunshine. Arizona has dry heat. The people of the Great Lakes have water. It is key to our transition from "The Rust Belt" to a world leader in innovation, economic prosperity, and sustainable growth. It differentiates us as a region.

As a result, I am adding my voice to the mayors of the Great Lakes and St. Lawrence Cities Initiative who are calling for Waukesha's application for diversion of Lake Michigan water to be denied.

Under the rules of the 2008 Compact and companion Agreement signed by the eight Great Lakes governors and two premiers of Canada, Great Lakes waters are not to be diverted from the Great Lakes Basin, with a few, limited exceptions. One of those exceptions can be made when a city outside the Basin, but located in a county that straddles the Basin, has exhausted all reasonable options for providing its community with clean, safe water.

The city of Waukesha has filed for a diversion based on that exception. However, by significantly expanding their future service area to include portions of Pewaukee, and the towns of Delafield, Genesee, and Waukesha—communities that have not demonstrated a need for Lake Michigan water—the city's leaders have created an application that is not in compliance with the Compact. In addition, according to an independent engineering report issued in 2015, another reasonable alternative exists for Waukesha's existing water service area. As a result, approving this application undermines the essence of the 2008 Compact and Agreement. It handcuffs the very people leading our cities into the future.

I remember the thrill of riding my bicycle on a path around the perimeter of Muskegon Lake last summer. A community once defined by sawmills and factories, Muskegon is reinventing itself as a recreation destination for outdoor enthusiasts like me. A shoreline of broken concrete, foundry slag, sheet metal, and slab wood is being softened, replaced with wetlands that attract fish, turtles, birds. The bike path showcases progress. The many public parks and beaches offer hope for new beginnings.

I recall jogging the Riverwalk of Detroit at the first hint of dawn, pausing to chat with a young African-American woman sharing her pride in the city block she, her husband, and neighbors are transforming into a floral showcase fit for a feature story in *Better Homes and Gardens*. I have walked the Flats of Cleveland, watched the sunset from the waterfront park in Windsor, jogged the miles of shoreline in Chicago, sailed into the bustling harbors of Milwaukee and Racine, and hiked the coastline from Gary, past Michigan City, and up to Benton Harbor. All are cities in transition. Across the region, mayors, city planners, members of the Chamber of Commerce, and local leaders are working hard to attract jobs, to provide ample opportunities for children and grandchildren, to make our cities safe, vibrant, and prosperous.

Water is one of our greatest differentiating assets in an increasingly competitive global environment. The 2008 agreements are designed to protect water for residents and businesses in the Great Lakes basin and those straddling communities who demonstrate dire need. This decision, the first application for a diversion, sets precedent. As a result, Waukesha leaders must demonstrate all reasonable efforts have been explored for providing water to the city, without the vastly expanded service area. Then, and only then, should a diversion of Lake Michigan water be considered.[21]

APRIL 2016 BLOG:
SAFELY SLATHERING SUNSCREEN

*L*ike many outdoor enthusiasts bearing the scars of skin cancer, I use copious amounts of suntan lotion. I didn't realize every time I jump in the lake or wash it off my body, I am potentially putting the health of Lake Michigan's ecosystem, as well as my own health, at risk.

The culprit is a microscopic particle of plastic called a microbead. A single container of sunscreen contains between ten trillion and one hundred trillion of these tiny culprits. So small they are impossible to see with the naked eye, microbeads began appearing in products like toothpastes, deodorants, face washes, shaving creams, and sunscreens in the 1990s. Used primarily to create a silky texture, they are also used as bulking agents, exfoliates, teeth polishers, and to prolong product shelf life.

Most of the time, the microbeads are rinsed off our bodies and flushed down the drain. Because the majority of water treatment plants cannot filter them, eventually the beads end up in surface waters like the Great Lakes. While some beads contain phthalates and bisphenol-A (BPA), chemicals linked to health issues, the majority of beads contain polypropylene or polyethylene. When the beads enter the waterways, they act as magnets, attracting other chemicals such as DDT (dichloro-diphenyl-trichloroethane), PAHs (polyaromatic hydrocarbons), and PCBs (polychlorinated biphenyls). The more chemicals the beads absorb, the bigger they become until eventually the beads are mistaken for food, ingested by fish and wildlife, and passed up the food chain to humans.

According to a study released by the State University of New York at Fredonia in 2013, there are 17,000 of these little balls of toxic chemicals in roughly one square foot of Lake Michigan water!

While little research is available that directly links microbeads to health risks in humans, there is certainly enough potential risk based on the chemicals either in the plastic beads or absorbed by them. Risks include cancer, damage to the liver, kidney, and nervous and reproductive systems. As a result, Congressional leaders worked across party lines in December 2015 to pass the Microbead-free Waters Act, legislation phasing out microbeads from personal care *rinse-off* products used to exfoliate or cleanse the skin and teeth. Products must be off retail shelves by 2019. Unfortunately, sunscreen is not considered a *rinse-off* product. If we want microbeads eliminated from *leave-on* products like lotions, it falls on the shoulders of consumers.

And so, I ask my reader to join me in scrutinizing the labels of favorite sunscreens and hand lotions. If the products contain polypropylene or polyethylene, call or email the manufacturer and voice your concern. I did. Within twenty-four hours, I was reading the company's commitment to "reflect not only the latest science and new regulations, but also consumer views and concerns."

If enough of us make this an issue, we can eliminate microbeads from the lotions we slather on our bodies and those of our children and grandchildren. We can help clean up our water.[22]

WINDS OF HOPE

"$\mathcal{A}$ fanatic is one who won't change his mind and can't change the subject."

Ellen Satterlee, then CEO of the Wege Foundation, quoted Winston Churchill to describe the late Peter Wege at the 2014 Healing Our Waters (HOW) Great Lakes Coalition annual meeting. Grounded in his passion for restoring the Great Lakes, Wege was fanatical when it came to his vision: "No single foundation, no single organization, no single nation will restore the Great Lakes by working alone. It will take partnerships among all who care for our magnificent Great Lakes to get the job done."

That fanaticism, combined with extraordinary leadership, were like faint ripples of hope skipping across the surface of a deteriorating Great Lakes ecosystem in 2004. Because of Peter Wege, twelve years later, the ripples are more like waves, one- to two-foot rollers curling alongside miles of shoreline and slowly eroding the cliffs of resistance.

Peter Wege died in July of 2014, two months before the HOW coalition held its tenth annual meeting in his beloved Grand Rapids. Working in concert with the region's mayors, governors, tribes, and business and industry leaders, the coalition is implementing a vision too powerful to shrug off, using a plan too grounded in science to dismiss, and relying on a team of fanatics too large, too resourceful, too dedicated to ignore.

Republicans and Democrats. Canadians and Americans. Staff and volunteers. Young and old.

Dreaming. Collaborating. Creating a healthier Great Lakes region.

I find myself remembering Mr. Wege's grandfatherly smile, his warm, welcoming handshake, and his words of deep, personal encouragement when I met him at the HOW conference in 2004. Upon learning I wrote the "Can One Person Make a Difference?" essay, read in the opening session of the Cleveland meeting, he made me feel as if I were a critical member of the team.

I suspect he made everyone feel that way. That's what it means to be a leader.

Between 2010 and 2016, more than $1.9 billion in federal Great Lakes Restoration Initiative (GLRI) monies have sponsored more than 2,500 projects, in concert with state and local government funds and private contributions. Many GLRI success stories are in Lake Michigan harbors we visit frequently.

Waukegan Harbor, once described as "the world's worst PCB (polychlorinated biphenyls) mess," was removed in 2014 from the list of forty-three Areas of Concern (AOCs) identified by the U.S. and Canadian governments in 1987.

White Lake, plagued for decades by excessive algae, loss of fish and wildlife habitat, excessive debris along the shores, and contaminated water that placed restrictions on fishing and drinking-water consumption, was one of Michigan's first AOC harbors to be delisted, removed as an AOC in November 2015.

Contaminated sediments have been removed from other AOCs, including Muskegon Lake, the Grand Calumet River in Indiana, and Wisconsin's Sheboygan, Milwaukee, and Kinnickinnic Rivers.

Wetlands and wildlife habitats are being restored throughout the basin, improving the water quality of watersheds, including our own Macatawa Watershed.

Dams are being eliminated, the natural flow of rivers restored, bank erosion reduced to improve fish habitat and recreational opportunities in areas like the Platte River near Frankfort and the Boardman River near Traverse City.

Invasive plants like phragmites, Japanese knotweed, purple loosestrife, and lyme grass are being removed from wetlands to return native plants and wildlife to the ecosystem alongside the Kalamazoo River and the Ozaukee Washington Land Trust, just north of Milwaukee. [23]

The exchange of information at these HOW conferences—the energy and friendships formed among this diverse and fanatical group of partners—is the essence of hope for our Great Lakes. I listen, pen in hand, as people discuss the challenges of storm water runoff affecting the water quality of Lake Erie and most watersheds in the region; the environmental risks associated with piping and the potential shipping of oil and tar sands from Canada to refineries in Indiana, Detroit, Sarnia, and Toledo; the decimation of the land caused by mining the pristine sand now used for fracking; the increasing number of sewage overflows resulting from heavy rains overpowering antiquated facilities; the invasion of the dreaded Asian carp; the delisting of the remaining AOCs; and the largely unknown effects of climate change.

It will take all of us—those who play in these waters, those whose business depends on these waters, those who drink these waters, those who feel the presence of God in these waters—to get the job done. We live in a democracy. We choose whether or not to lift our sails to the winds of hope, opportunities, and dreams.

We choose.

SEEKING BALANCE

The challenge in sailing is finding the balance in the wind, the sails, the waves, any underwater current, and the pull from the hull or the rudder. When one discovers that "sweet spot," one can sail the boat in a straight line, making the most progress while expending the least amount of energy.

And so it is in life.

THE GIFT OF FEEDBACK

*I*n corporate life, I received what was called "360-degree feedback" every year. While ideally feedback is ongoing, the structured review process ensured managers were receiving feedback from all members of their team on a regular basis.

"Feedback is a gift," I remember being told by one of my mentors. "For how do you fix something if you don't know it's broken?"

The most difficult thing about my new life as a writer, photographer, and advocate for the Great Lakes is the lack of feedback. The traditional publishing business is in the throes of upheaval as readers move to new platforms created by the Internet. And yet, these publishers continue to be inundated with submissions by writers like myself. Occasionally my work is picked up, and I'm euphoric for a week or two. But then there is silence. Deafening and discouraging. The dragons of self-doubt emerge from the shadows.

Until I began blogging. To my surprise, readers are eager to give me feedback. And thanks to friends, neighbors, and others involved in restoring the Great Lakes, my audience of readers is mushrooming, first on my website, then on Facebook. Some publicly post comments; the majority send me emails. I am now dialoguing with people I have never met—all over the country.

And this is what I am learning . . . People do care about this magnificent body of water called the Great Lakes. They find it difficult to stay abreast of the issues. Like Rubin, they want to understand the science—have the facts behind the story. And they are willing to get involved. They are also swamped with their own priorities. The easier I can make it for them to engage, the more likely they will do so. I also realize they want to share in the beauty, the adventure, the romance of the Great Lakes, as well as the challenges. The art *and* the science.

Within those guideposts, I am limited only by my own imagination. And that is the greatest gift of all.

BATTLE SCARS

*T*he sun is already warming the dewy mist of a late September morning as streaks of light cut across patchy skies. Tomorrow, the boat will be hoisted from the water and placed in a metal cradle for winter. I am excited to get to the marina, to trot one last time down the pier and perch myself in my favorite spot in the cockpit. Stretched behind the wheel with a computer on my lap, I plan to spend the day writing stories, inspired by the soothing sound of waves slapping against the hull, the occasional splash of a salmon gulping a final breath before heading upstream, the geese squawking overhead as they jockey for positions in their V-shaped formation.

My mind is spinning with the seeds for a blog as I slide my feet into a pair of "mules," leather topsiders designed for boaters. They are closest to the door and the ones I absentmindedly choose to wear on my final day of the boating season.

The afternoon does not disappoint. The sun, robbed of its summer intensity, still skips across the water, flirting with the cool autumn breeze. A few lingering barn swallows light momentarily on dock lines; they are skittish after a season of being sprayed with a hose and swooshed away. But today they are safe. Rubin is absorbed in readying the boat for pullout. At the moment, he is focused on unscrewing one of the giant (four-foot-long) teak benches from the cockpit. The other bench stands on end, ready to be hauled to the waiting cart, wheeled to the car, and then taken home to be refinished. Like painting, refinishing the teak is my job.

"No paintbrush fits my hand," Rubin told me after we first married. Engineering is his specialty. Slave labor has become mine.

The sun is just beginning its descent on this last day on the water, a time we traditionally pause to celebrate the completion of another safe boating season. I close the computer and slide my feet into the mules, forgetting that the soles have hardened with age, the shoes demoted to yard work earlier in the season because they are too slick for boating. And then I do what any good crew would do. I grab the bulky seat to lug it to the cart.

My left foot stretches for the dock, a move as automatic as getting out of bed. But today, the instant the mule touches the dock, it skids across the boards like a skate on ice.

Immediately, I seize the handrail on the nearby post with my right hand to keep from falling, with the left still awkwardly clutching the heavy bench. I try to regain my balance, but the weight on my right foot is pushing the boat away from the pier. For a moment I straddle the water before the right foot slides off the boat and my leg crashes into the wooden corner of a twelve-foot fender board.

Pain shoots up my right leg like fire ripping across dune grass. Taking a deep breath, I pull myself up with my right hand, the left still clutching the bench, and then crumple in a heap on the dock. Immediately my mind takes control, blocking all pain, all emotion. As if a distant third-party observer, I turn over and stare at the L-shaped, jagged gash cutting across my right shin. The tear is deep enough to see bone, edged in red but without pools of blood. It will need stitches, of course. But like the scar two inches higher, remnants of a surgery to remove a cancerous squamous cell, the wound will be difficult to sew because there is so little flesh stretched across that part of the leg. Most likely it will leave another large, permanent scar.

Thoughts flow through me in slow motion.

My legs ground me to the earth, pillars of strength carrying me through life. Jogging legs. On these joints I have explored cities, deserts, bogs, sand dunes, mountains, beaches, glaciers, farmland, and marshes. I have seen the glossy yellow petals of the buttercup, the snow-white whiskers of the Canada violet, the red feather cap of a Gila woodpecker. I have stood on the edge of a summer rain and sniffed the crisp scent of a creosote bush in the desert, smelled the freshness of a forest, inhaled the salty air of an ocean.

But life is more than discoveries, celebration, and thanksgiving. These legs have also borne the weight of a suffering heart, supported me as faces I have treasured disappear from my life. Death. Accidents. Illnesses. Geography. Misunderstandings. Divergent paths. The older I get, the more loss seems to be heaped upon my shoulders. And so, on the balls of these feet, I have learned to pray and listen for the whisper of angels.

I fear I have taken these legs for granted.

Unaware of my fall, Rubin continues to remove screws from the other bench.

"Rubin, help," I say in a scratchy whisper. And he is there, immediately, as he has been since the day I challenged him to a game of racquetball.

The repair requires thirteen stitches, a special wound-management procedure for one allergic to antibiotic ointments, latex, and adhesives, and two long months without jogging. Like the cracks in the fiberglass of our aging boat, the scar will be visible forever. But it is just a surface scar, not structural. And I feel fortunate.

In hindsight, there was no excuse for wearing the wrong shoes to the boat. It was just a moment when my thoughts drifted away from the present, when my mind was preoccupied with my own internal chatter. But isn't that frequently the root cause of scars? Those we inflict on ourselves . . . and on others?

Hobbling from the emergency-room wheelchair to the backseat of the car, I murmur three words: "To the boat." Rubin doesn't argue.

By the time we arrive, the lake is a glassy sheet of black with only a hint of pink shading the evening's skies. We say a prayer of thanks that my injury is not more serious and toast the season, the lake, the boat, each other.

"And here's to throwing out every pair of old boating shoes," Rubin adds.

Of course, I don't. The upper leather on the shoes is still perfect. And I do need yard shoes.

WHY AM I MARCHING?

*D*riving through dense fog Saturday morning, I asked myself, *Why?* Why, after decades of avoiding political marches and rallies, was I joining the Women's March of 2017?

As I drove, I found myself humming the tunes from Lin-Manuel Miranda's Broadway performance of *Hamilton*, particularly the lyrics where Alexander Hamilton chides Aaron Burr for always remaining on the sidelines, for refusing to take a stand.

What was I willing to stand for?

I arrived early, never dreaming that I would be one of 8,000 people to rally on the steps of Michigan's capitol or that I would be one of 2.5 million who would gather across the world on Saturday, January 21, 2017. Women—and a few men—mulled about the grounds, chatting freely, quietly with complete strangers. Each braved the gray, misty air for a different reason.

"I came because I believe in democracy," a woman told me. "And that means having the freedom to gather, to march, to protest. I'm here because I believe in our country."

The plethora of colorful signs highlighted the issue each held closest to her heart: women's rights, the rights of people of color and of different religious preferences, access to healthcare, the importance of public education, concerns about climate change, the rights of the LBGT communities, a woman's right to choose, and those believing in pro-life.

This was not a march "against" as much as it was a march "for" those things people hold dear.

"One and a half years ago I was diagnosed with cancer," a striking twenty-two-year-old man told the audience. At the time, he had just graduated from Eastern Michigan University and did not have a job. After months of chemotherapy, bone-marrow testing, and multiple hospital stays, his healthcare expenses exceeded $400,000. Fortunately, under the Affordable Care Act, he was a rider on his parent's insurance plan. But what will he do if the act is repealed? Even though he is now cancer-free, will he be denied insurance because of a pre-existing condition?

Another woman in her early twenties spoke about the importance of continuing to fund Planned Parenthood.

"I was eighteen, pregnant, and scared," she told the group, her voice shaking with emotion. She and her boyfriend went to Planned Parenthood so she could get an abortion. And yet, once inside the facility, 100% of the focus was on her health and that of the baby's. As a result of the care she received, she decided to keep the baby. She opted to become a mother.

Everyone had a story. What was mine?

As the rally neared its end, a streak of sun finally cut through the fog, showering its light on the dome, the flags of our country and state, and the thousands of faces below. In that moment, I knew.

E pluribus unum. "Out of many, one."

We are a country of immigrants and descendants of immigrants. Me, included. In the mid-1800s, people of my ethnic origin faced "NINA" signs, "No Irish Need Apply," when they immigrated to the United States, hoping to build a future for themselves and their families. By the time I was born, I faced none of that. But thanks to my (largely) Irish parents, thousands of students across all ethnicities and socioeconomic backgrounds received an education that helped prepare them for their future, for the future of their families.

My mother, formerly the public information director for the East Lansing Public School system, helped pass the millage to fund education for the community's students the eighteen years she was in that position. My father, a professor at Michigan State University, focused on obtaining funding for postsecondary education—community colleges and schools of technology as well as colleges and universities. He believed every child deserved a chance to create a better life. Every child—regardless of color or wealth or status.

Not surprisingly, I believe in inclusion and was fortunate to be a senior executive for a company that emphasized "sustainable profits," long-term success that required tapping the creativity and mindsets of a diverse, global population of employees. The company was, and is, successful—a leader in its field. As a result, I was able to retire at an early age, to recreate myself as a writer, to focus my efforts on ensuring everyone—everyone—has access to clean, safe drinking water. Particularly everyone living in the Great Lakes region.

I am marching because I believe in the fundamental principles of our democracy, including the separation of three distinct branches of government. I am marching because I believe in negotiated compromises that allow us to bridge our differences and build better futures for all of us. I am marching because I believe in a free press that keeps us informed, as citizens in a democracy. I am marching because I want diversity to make our country's decisions richer, more sustainable, more successful. I am marching because all citizens, regardless of color or background, should be allowed to participate in the decisions of this country, should be allowed to march, must be allowed to vote.

I am marching because I can.

That is a right worth marching for.

MY HAND IN YOURS

I slide my hand in Rubin's as we walk alongside Ludington's Municipal Marina, heading toward the beach. The sun is warming a chilly July morning and there is not a breath of air. Glancing over at our boat docked in the marina, I notice the small, navy-blue pennant hanging limply beneath the boat's spreaders. A sign.

We support the Great Lakes.

In my other hand, I finger a blue marble, a smooth glass surface sparkling like a drop of water in the sunlight. Rolling the marble between my thumb and forefinger, I reflect on my life-long relationship with Lake Michigan.

On many levels, this lake defines me . . . us. It is why, on this morning of July 3, 2017, Rubin and I are joining hundreds of thousands of people, perhaps millions, joining hands alongside the 10,900 miles of Great Lakes shoreline. We are part of a human chain. A sign. Despite our diverse backgrounds and experiences,

our different political affiliations, we stand united when it comes
to these lakes.

We want them healthy.

"Love them, protect them, link hands for them," Kimberly
Simon shared with me. The mastermind behind the "All Hands
On Deck" July 3ʳᵈ celebration, Kimberly had no experience in
political advocacy until she learned that the funding for the Great
Lakes Restoration Initiative had been eliminated in the Trump
Administration's Fiscal 2018 budget.

"I promised myself I would learn how to write letters, make
phone calls, and let the politicians know these lakes are important,"
said the retired art teacher from Charlevoix, Michigan. "But I
wanted to do more. I wanted to create something positive to draw
us together, something uplifting, something that would be good
for the soul. I had this vision of people joining hands across the
entire shoreline of the Great Lakes, united in support of our water."

She began sharing her vision with others. In less than a month,
more than 1300 volunteers and thirty-two leaders, or "Captains" as
she calls those spearheading community-wide celebrations, joined
the team transitioning that vision into reality.

I am grateful there is a gathering in Ludington, the harbor into
which we sailed last evening. In many communities, participants
will drop a blue marble, with their memories, into a bowl, exchanging their memories for another's. It is why I am carrying a marble,
why Rubin has one in his pocket. And while our memories are
different, the deep connection with the Great Lakes is something
millions of people across eight states and two Canadian provinces
have in common.

"What is your favorite memory of the Great Lakes?" I ask Rubin.

"Wave-hopping in *Indy*," he replies immediately.

I stop and look up at him dumbfounded.

"Remember?" he continues. "We took our first dinghy wave-hopping in eight-foot rollers when we lived in Wisconsin. Remember flying over the top of the waves and crashing into the troughs? Remember we broke the floor boards?"

"Of course, I remember. But seriously? That's your favorite?"

He grins. "What's yours?"

Silently I begin scrolling through a relationship with these lakes that is as diverse, as physical, emotional, and spiritual as the relationship I have with the man at my side. So many memories, it is hard to choose a favorite.

We walk in silence past the old Coast Guard station, past the place on the beach where I once spotted, photographed, and reported a patch of the invasive baby's breath. We pause briefly, as we always do, when the Ludington Light comes into view. We have sailed through this channel in the pink hush of sunrise, but also in the wild fury of a Lake Michigan gale.

All five of the Great Lakes—but particularly this one—have fostered an intimacy between us. We have learned to pause and appreciate the many moods of nature while walking alongside their shores. We have learned to anticipate each other's needs, to speak forcefully, but gently, in order to survive the lakes' most wicked storms. We have learned to negotiate our differences, to laugh at our adventures, to love our time together—particularly the ritual of sharing sunrises and sunsets over the water. The lakes have taught us what it means to be a team.

A crowd of people is assembling on the public beach, the site of Ludington's "All Hands on Deck" celebration. Before joining them, I stop and look into those engaging blue eyes of the man whose hand remains in mine.

"My favorite memory occurred thirty-seven years ago, when we stood on the Milwaukee shoreline and you told me you'd prefer to live alongside Lake Michigan, rather than the west coast. That was the moment I knew we were soulmates."

He leans over and lightly kisses my cheek.

Walking to the edge of the water, we join hands with strangers to become part of a massive human chain, to stand united in our commitment to prioritize and protect the Great Lakes, to send a message to the politicians.

It is a memory I will carry with me forever.

You are not a drop in the ocean, you are the ocean in a drop, wrote the thirteenth-century poet Rumi.

Or, perhaps we are the Great Lakes in a marble.

SEARCHING FOR A BRIDGE
ACROSS A BASIN

*I*t is the mouth of the Kalamazoo River, west of Saugatuck, that currently troubles me. Upstream, the Environmental Protection Agency continues cleanup efforts at the Allied Paper Superfund site. And while it took four years and more than $1.2 billion, Enbridge completed its cleanup of the river after its oil pipeline ruptured in 2010.

But where the river flows into Lake Michigan, once again, litigation dominates the headlines regarding the development of 310 acres of pristine coastal habitat just north of the river. Money that could have been invested in furthering efforts to restore one of the most impaired waterways in the Great Lakes instead pads the pockets of attorneys.

There has to be a better way than ongoing litigation.

I, like many, hoped we could pool enough public and private funds to purchase roughly 500 acres of the former Denison property in 2006; to place this pristine coastal land bordering both sides of the Kalamazoo River mouth in the hands of the public. It did not happen. An out-of-towner named Aubrey McClendon won the bid. And while he eventually sold the 173 acres on the south side of the river, allowing for the creation of the Saugatuck Harbor Natural Area, his plans for the north side splintered the community and nearly bankrupted the township as litigation dragged on for years.

I added my voice to those fighting McClendon's plans to place an equestrian center, a marina, multi-story hotel, golf course, shops, condominiums, and residential homes on the land. My concern was the effect it would have on the river as it flowed into Lake Michigan. Manure from horse barns, fertilizers used on lawns and fairways, runoff from asphalt roads and parking lots would hurt, not help, the region-wide efforts to restore the Great Lakes.

McClendon died in March of 2016. Once again, I hoped we might pool public and private resources to purchase the land. I had a vision of one day hiking the trails threading through the forested backdunes of the Saugatuck Dunes State Park to the riverbed of the Kalamazoo River. I envisioned a short, flat, eco-friendly Riverwalk that would make the lake more accessible to the elderly and families with very small children. One day, kayakers and canoeists exploring the coast of Lake Michigan by day could easily access the potpourri of harbor communities in the evening, camping in state parks that included Saugatuck State Park. The former Denison house on the north side of the river mouth might become a place where we integrated innovation, science, technology, and the environment—perhaps similar to the Discovery World facility adjacent to the Lakeshore State Park in Milwaukee—only with a West Michigan focus on the world's largest freshwater dune system.

Above all, I hoped preserving this pristine coastal land would aid efforts to remove the Kalamazoo River from the government's list of most toxic waterways.

But we, the public, did not purchase the land.

As of January 2017, there are new owners. They plan to place two thirds of the land, roughly 203 acres, in a conservation easement. To make that economically possible, they plan to build seven homes alongside Lake Michigan and eight alongside the Kalamazoo River, and dig a 1500-foot-long private boat basin with twenty-three home sites on the land where the former Broward Marine building used to stand.

The proposed 18'-deep basin is at the heart of the current litigation. The Saugatuck Dune Coastal Alliance, a nonprofit conservation organization, filed suit against the Saugatuck Township Planning Commission in June, claiming preliminary approval for the basin (still subject to review by the U.S. Amy Corps of Engineers and the Michigan Department of Environmental Quality) was in violation of the township's approval process and zoning ordinances.

I have stood alongside one of the initial leaders of the Saugatuck Dune Coastal Alliance at numerous public hearings when McClendon owned the property. She is a published author and poet, a woman of heart, a nurturing spirit. She, and others, are volunteering their time and money, trying to do the right thing for a fragile ecosystem at the mouth of an already-impaired river.

I know one of the new owners. A published poet, she, too, is a woman of heart, a nurturing spirit. She and her partners are also trying to do the right thing. And while this new plan is nothing like McClendon's, I can see both sides of a familiar question.

How do we, as neighbors, friends, and acquaintances sharing this special place on the planet, negotiate a balance between protecting our water and allowing development that provides jobs and economic prosperity to the community? Is it better for the ecosystem to preserve two thirds of the land and dig a basin or fully develop the property with home sites and roads crisscrossing the dunes?

I don't know the answer. I doubt a judge will, either.

Litigation is the face of mistrust, lost faith in government's ability to find that delicate balance between jobs and the environment. Particularly in today's political realities, where it appears scarce natural resources are neither valued nor protected, I share the frustration, the suspicions, the anger of members of this grassroots organization fighting to protect the life and land they hold dear. In this small resort community, I wish we could find a way to mediate our differences without litigating every step we are making together as stewards of this planet, without pouring limited financial resources into attorney fees.

But trust, once broken, is hard to repair. And I fear I am looking for a bridge that does not exist. Yet.

NOVEMBER 2017 BLOG:
WHY IS DIALOGUE SO DIFFICULT?

I have anguished over how best to advocate for the Great Lakes without contributing to the polarization ripping apart our communities, our country, and our planet.

Last month, I attended the Michigan Department of Environmental Quality's public hearing on the proposed development for the north side of the Kalamazoo River mouth. I attended the meeting because, while it is tempting to depend on the many nonprofit organizations advocating for the water, in my gut, I knew I must be there, too. That is what it means to live in a democracy. I am "We, the people . . ."

I came hoping to hear examples of the developer's claims, outlined on the NorthShore of Saugatuck website, for living in harmony with the environment. Instead, I heard how metal plates will be pounded into the dunes, how more than 240,000 cubic yards of sand will be excavated, and how much of that sand—once the floor beneath a boat manufacturer and potentially contaminated with epoxies, solvents, and other chemicals—will be spread on the beach adjacent to the Saugatuck Dunes State Park. I wanted to believe the language on the website, tried to remember the owners' commitment to preserve two thirds of the land, but I struggled to keep from despair.

I was equally disappointed in the comments made by those opposing the development—not all, certainly, but many. I listened to people insist the creation of the basin be denied because of the environmental irresponsibility of boaters and the reckless, destructive behavior of the wealthy and their children. So many labels. So much prejudice.

I left the public hearing depleted of energy.

The poet Rumi wrote:

*Out beyond the ideas of wrongdoing and rightdoing,
there is a field. I'll meet you there.*

There is no "field" for dialogue in the formal approval process, no place for the principals to exchange opposing views in a constructive manner that leads to honest, fact-based discussions, compromise, and resolutions that move our relationships and our community forward.

Even if there was such a place, dialogue is difficult.

Marshall Rosenberg explains in his book *Nonviolent Communication: A Language of Life* that we have learned many forms of "life-alienating communication" that injure ourselves and others. Through its emphasis on deep listening, nonviolent communication fosters respect, attentiveness, and empathy as it creates "a language of compassion."

"The key to finding creative space for dialogue in an adversarial situation is to look for common needs," explained Lisa Gottlieb, a nonviolent communication-certified trainer. "All parties want to be heard, know their needs matter. I suspect the property owners want to recoup their investment, want financial stability and safety, a sense of predictability. Most people, certainly those who have taken out a mortgage or loan, understand this.

"While those opposed to the development are arguing for the preservation of the dunes, the water, and the wildlife," she continued, "it is also in the best interest of the owners to protect the natural resources that make the property valuable."

While both sides may have different strategies, searching for the similarity in needs is the first step in any conflict resolution.

"If I get too caught up in what I see as the outcome, I lose my capacity to care for another," Gottlieb said. "The owners become 'monsters' interested only in making money. Those opposed become 'tree huggers who aren't interested in fair business interests.' People feel attacked. Values and blame get in the way of finding common strategies. This is not easy. It takes lots of work and a willingness to be curious, to want to learn from one another."

The public hearing was not a place for such creative listening and learning. And while that saddens me, it is outside my sphere of influence. But I can learn this new language of compassion, change the way I communicate.

Perhaps one day there will be a "field." I promise to meet you there and listen—without judgement—to understand your needs, empathize, and engage in conversation that taps my heart as well as my mind. I hope you will be there, too.[24]

"JUST THE WAY YOU ARE"

*I*t isn't late-stage breast cancer. It isn't the possibility of paralysis after a horrific automobile accident. It isn't the slow neurological decline of multiple sclerosis. But it is change, the restructuring of a lifetime physical image created by me so that I might learn to love and accept myself. It is the mental photograph of a blond-haired, blue-eyed, trim, tan, athletic woman who lives to be outdoors. All of that can still be true save one. "Tan" needs to be permanently erased from the picture.

It seems silly. It should be easy to resolve. For me, it is neither silly nor easy.

After eight surgeries to remove cancerous squamous cells most likely caused by chronic exposure to the sun, I know immediately when I see it. A fast-growing red bump on my skin with a white cauliflower center. Cancer.

The sun, that dearest of friends, that golden ball of light that breathes life into the earth's frosty floor, that warms a body chilled by the biting winds of April and creates the glittering diamonds frolicking across Lake Michigan, has betrayed me.

Betrayed me. For the sun that has kissed and caressed my body for decades has silently, secretly, tainted my skin with poison.

How can that which nourishes also harm?

"We can continue to cut and piece you together," I remember the plastic surgeon at Chicago's Northwestern Memorial Hospital telling me after my second procedure. "Or you can decide to do something to care for your body."

I looked for reasons to deny the obvious. As a teenager, had I not swathed my body in baby oil and sprawled on aluminum foil to maximize the intensity of the sun? Had I not read that most damage is done early, before I began smearing sunblock all over my body? Had my fourth surgery not confirmed my belief—the incision to remove the cancer sliced high across the thigh, a part of my body that had not seen sunlight in decades? Surely, I was managing the sun's potential death siren to my pale Irish body. But so many heartbreaking diagnoses. So many incisions. It was time to face reality.

Underneath this wide-brim hat, long-sleeved SPF 30 shirt, lightweight pants, and sunglasses lies a free-spirited rebel who is struggling. I stare at the sparkling pathway of light, extending like a road across the water from the golden ball of the sun to the stern of our sailboat. I long to duck below and rip this new clothing from my body, to feel once again the kiss of the breeze and the hot touch of day's light on my skin. I want to try again to liberally spread sunblock all over my body, so I can don a pair of shorts and a sleeveless T-shirt . . . so I can once again be me.

But all temptation has been removed from my wardrobe, including the mules. Accidents, illness, and aging happen to us all. Even me.

It is Rubin who is re-outfitting me, scouring online sites and stores to find lightweight, comfortable, sun-resistant attire . . . on sale. He enjoys clothing me in fashion. For most of my life, he has accompanied me on dreaded trips to stores to find dresses, shoes, slacks, and tops for work, weddings, funerals. When he selects the attire, people notice. Friends say with love and laughter, "Oh, Rubin must have chosen that! It's gorgeous."

It is my captain, my boataholic husband, and the man I love more than anyone on this earth who is helping me transition to this new woman who lives to be in the outdoors—safely.

The sun, once a fist above the shore, is dissolving into the golden streaks of sunset. I reach across the cockpit for his hand and squeeze it gently. Someday with misty eyes and a sad heart, I will help him hang a "For Sale" sign over the stern rail of *Balance*. For he, too, must be safe. Together we will climb on and off dozens of boats, looking for our next piece of waterfront property. Most likely, it will be a newer sailboat or trawler with push buttons for anchoring, bow thrusters for docking, something easier to maneuver and ideal for those with gray hairs and wrinkly, scarred skin.

Someday the stern of our boat will read, *The Inevitable II*.

But that day is not today. And as the skies begin to darken and the pinpoint light of Venus appears on the horizon, I take off my hat, run fingers through my head of hair, and ask Rubin, "Do I have hat head?"

Slowing shaking his head from side to side, a hint of a smile touching his face, he takes my hand in his and whispers, "I love you just the way you are."

EPILOGUE

I find writing to be both a skill and an art, forcing me to dig deep inside myself and marry the voice of my mind with that of my heart. It is scary stuff, difficult, but also rewarding. And while my college backpack—post Africa—was stuffed with books on finance, economics, marketing, statistics, and accounting, I realize now, in my later years, that writing is a gift entrusted to me at birth. My responsibility is to use it to make a difference, to engage others in helping to restore and protect the scarcest resource on this planet.

But there are many forms of writing. And since *A Child's Garden of Verses*, a book of poems, first kindled my interest in writing as a child, I am now learning to write poetry with the help of Jack Ridl, an award-winning poet, former Hope College professor, and friend. Unquestionably, the classes are pushing me outside my comfort zone. But that's how I learn. Influenced by parents who believed strongly in education, I know learning, for me, is life.

My first assignment with Jack was to write a poem titled "In My Time Capsule." The first line of the poem was to be "I would place…" To my surprise, when I sat down to write the poem, words tumbled onto the page that explain why I am willing to learn the chemistry behind microbeads, study public-trust doctrine, listen to farmers describe the challenges of competing in a global environment, understand the science behind treating ballast water to prevent the spread of aquatic invasive species, read legislation that affects our water, our air, and our land, and understand why I am willing to write and speak publicly about all I am learning. And so, with great humility, I share with you one of the first poems I have written. It is a whisper from my heart to yours.

IN MY TIME CAPSULE

I would place…
a tablespoon of clear,
clean water from the depths
of my beloved lake,
a crumbled leaf
from the disappearing ash,
a powdery white feather
from the piping plover,
the scrappy branch
of a Pitcher's thistle.

On second thought…

I will fill the capsule
with my teeth-grinding
worry that nature's

treasures are disappearing;
add the moments
of debilitating despair,
the fleeting flashes of cynicism,
and all negative energy
that tempts silence, apathy,
my own death.

And then . . .

I will wander in wonder
alongside that lake,
reveling in the glories
of each holy moment,
adding my voice
to the hope-filled chatter
of the finches and chickadees
flittering about the forest,
the seagulls and sanderlings
scavenging the beach.

ACKNOWLEDGMENTS

The woman who first introduced me to writing, whose own life as a journalist, published author, and poet has been an inspiration since childhood, is my mother. She critiqued this manuscript several times, encouraging me when the process of publishing seemed overwhelming. She and my dad planted the seeds that allowed me to recreate my life as a writer, photographer, and Great Lakes advocate. Without their loving support over the decades, I would not be the person I am today.

It takes an unusual and very special friend to scour through a manuscript several times so as to provide honest, constructive feedback. In my case, I am fortunate to have Jean Bergman, Kris Kennedy, Elaine McKeough, Mary Ellen Miller, Eric Stemle, and Chuck and Ruth Watts in my life. Also cheering me along as I recreated the second half of my life are my coaches and mentors, Grace Menzel, Alene Moris, Jack Ridl, and Tracy Wimberly. Thank you for believing in me and investing your time in my life's work.

Scheduling talks and/or providing me constant insight into their own work and passion regarding the Great Lakes ecosystem are Elizabeth Brockwell-Tillman, Dave Dempsey, David Hamilton, Amy Heilman, Tracey Shafroth, Alan Steinman, David and Alison Swan, and David Ullrich. And when I was about to give up on ever publishing the book, I received a giant nudge from author Jerry Dennis and fellow members of the 2016 Bear River Writers' Conference.

I am forever indebted to the many friends who have encouraged me through this often-difficult transition from businesswoman to Great Lakes advocate. Your willingness to listen, provide insight, and support me through the good times and tough ones are gifts I hope to always offer you in return. Thank you, too, to the readers regularly commenting on my blog and Facebook pages. It helps knowing someone is out there when I post my thoughts on the Internet. My thanks to the editors of *Sail* magazine, who published earlier versions of "Autumn Crossing" and "Seeking Common Ground," *Michigan Blue*, for publishing "Winter Walks," and *The Holland Sentinel*, for hiring me to write a monthly column on the Great Lakes. Thanks to my sister, Helen McKinney, for her proofreading and editorial support and to Paloma Havlik for her creative work on the 14 KARAT BOOKS logo and for taking my publicity photograph.

But the person to whom I owe the greatest gratitude is the boataholic, captain, husband, and best friend in my life, Rubin. He not only allowed but also encouraged me to share the stories about our life together so that others might experience the Great Lakes and join us in celebrating and protecting them. I am truly blessed that he opened the door to the chapel that day, inviting me to spend my life with him.

GLOSSARY

Aft ▸ Backside. Toward the stern. For example, the aft cabin is the back cabin.

Anchor Etiquette ▸ Includes not anchoring in close proximity to another when an entire bay is available; not recharging the generator during the evening cocktail hour as the sun romantically slips below the horizon; not blasting one's music throughout the uninhabited island, off which you have settled for the day; not bunching up the anchor line and throwing it and the anchor into the water with the hope it sticks.

Apparent Wind ▸ The wind one feels when standing on deck. It is NOT the same as true wind. I wish there was an easy explanation. There isn't. Apparent wind is a combination of boat speed and the angle of the boat to the true wind. For the record, the wind I feel is whatever I see on the instrument panel—with the hope it is set to whatever measurement the captain uses to make good decisions.

Backdune ▸ Farthest from the lake and protected from wind and waves by rolling hills of sand called foredunes, the backdunes eventually become forested mountains of sand that provide an inspiring and exhilarating backdrop to an outdoor workout.

Bimini ▸ Canvas covering the cockpit of a boat, protecting one from sun and rain. Rarely used on our boat until now, until learning the sun, which nurtures, also harms.

Bow ▸ Front of the boat and a great place to stand when the lake is flat and the breeze mild, provided one hangs on to the lifelines so the speed and accuracy of the "overboard" drill is never tested.

Burgee ▸ Three-pointed flags, typically representing a yacht club or organization with which the owner is affiliated. In our case, since careers made us gypsies, we fly six: Bay City Yacht Club, Racine Yacht Club, Sandusky Yacht Club, two Macatawa Bay Yacht Club burgees representing different eras, and a Bayshore Yacht Club burgee. We also fly a Michigan State University flag during football season, and a navy-blue pennant representing our support for a healthy Great Lakes ecosystem.

Butt bucket ▸ A colorful, diaper-like contraption that clips to the trapeze line dangling from the mast of daysailers, allowing one to balance the boat by leaning back over the windward side. Unquestionably, the most unflattering sailing attire on the planet.

Catamaran ▸ A two-hulled boat which, if shorter than twenty feet, is sure to drench crew and captain in heavy air. But it's fast! Much faster than a monohull—a single-hulled boat.

Cleat ▸ A fitting to which one ties mooring lines to keep the boat safely and securely nestled in a slip.

Cunningham ▸ A line on the front of the mainsail used to eliminate the wrinkles or "luff" of the sail.

Downwind ▸ Also called "running," it means sailing with the wind directly at your back. It can be the most dangerous course, as the wind can easily catch the sails and slam them to the other side. Sailing downwind is also the warmest sail and most likely to attract flies. Have a flyswatter on deck.

Dune, Linear ▸ Parallel ridges of sand that formed as lake levels dropped over the last 5,000 years. Also called dune and swale complexes, they define the coast of the Indiana Dunes and Michigan's Wilderness State Park and are typically fifteen feet high.

Dune, Parabolic ▸ Dunes found along the southeastern coast of Lake Michigan. Formed by wind, waves, and high lake levels, they can tower more than 200′ high and are best identified by their large, U-shaped blowouts—open, shifting valleys of sand.

Dune, Perched ▸ Dunes perched on top of glacial moraine bluffs. Most well-known are Sleeping Bear Dunes off the northeastern coast of Lake Michigan and Grand Sable on Lake Superior.

Falling Off ▸ One cannot steer directly into the wind and so must turn the boat away from the wind (or fall off) to sail forward. Sailing as close to the wind as possible, called close-hauled, pointing, or beating into the wind is usually the shortest distance to reaching the first mark in a race.

Foredune ▸ Rolling hills of sand alongside the beach, usually dotted with beach grass.

Galley ▸ The kitchen. Appliances may be slim, but there is always a cooler for cocktails.

Genoa ▸ A genoa is the giant headsail. GG. Giant/Genoa.

Halyard ▸ Lines that hoist sails up the mast. HH. Halyards hoist.

Head ▸ The bathroom on a boat where one must never use more than four tiny squares of flimsy, dissolvable toilet paper designed for boats. If one needs more than four squares, find a marina.

Headsail ▸ The sail "ahead" of the mast. Different-size headsails have different names. A Genoa, the largest headsail, is hoisted during light air. Smaller jibs are used in heavy air. Cruising boats like ours have a roller furling headsail, meaning the sail rolls into the forestay and the size can be adjusted according to conditions. A "handkerchief" would be similar to a storm jib on a racing boat.

Heel ▸ When the wind fills the sail, and the boat begins tipping to one side. Seats on the high side, the windward side, are the most comfortable and typically where the "railmeat" are stationed during a race.

Interdunal trough ▸ The valleys forming between the foredunes and backdunes. The troughs can house ponds of freshwater called interdunal ponds.

Jib ▸ The smaller headsails.

Jibe ▸ Changing the course heading on a sailboat by turning the boat when the wind is off the stern. The boom tends to swing rapidly across the cockpit, so duck!

Keel ▸ The heavier the better, as it stretches below the hull to keep the boat from flipping. On older boats like ours, the depth of the keel can be problematic in the shallower channels and harbors.

Knot ▸ One nautical mile per hour. 1 nautical mile = 1.852 km = 1.15078 miles. We set all instruments in nautical miles.

Lazarette ▸ External lockers in the stern, never quite large enough to hold anything neatly.

Leeward ▸ Away from the wind. For example, when heeling in heavy air, the leeward side is the side where the toe rail is closest to the water.

Lifeline ▸ Plastic-covered stainless steel lines designed to keep one from falling overboard. Hold on to these when moving about the boat to prevent the dreaded "overboard" drill.

Luff ▸ Allowing the sails to flap in the air to slow the boat, is called "luffing" the sails. The "luff" also defines the front edge of a sail.

Mainsail ▸ The sail hoisted up the aft side of the mast.

Overboard Drill ▸ Throw the ring buoy (preferably line attached) as close as possible to the one in the water. Turn on the motor. Point into the wind. Drop the sails. Flip the ladder down. Circle back to the person. Take the motor out of gear as the person nears the boat. Help them aboard.

Port ▸ The left side of the boat. Easy to remember because there are four letters in LEFT, four letters in PORT.

Pulpit ▸ Stainless-steel railings across the bow and stern.

Railmeat ▸ Those too heavy to work foredeck, too weak to control the mainsheet, too inexperienced to call tactics, too poor to be at the helm. Their job on a race is to plunk their bodies on the windward side and dangle their feet in the spray.

Reach, Beam ▸ Sailing perpendicular to the wind, or roughly 90 degrees off the wind.

Reach, Broad ▸ Sailing midway between a beam reach and downwind or approximately 135 degrees off the wind

Reach, Close ▸ Midway between sailing a close-hauled course and a beam reach. Usually the fastest point of sail.

Ropes ▸ Do not exist on a boat. If in doubt, call it a "line," and describe it... e.g., the red line with white spots, the white line with red spots, the blue line. Most lines are color-coded because only the diehards (like Rubin) can remember all the names.

Shackle ▸ Metal fitting with pin and ring guaranteed to destroy one's fingernails.

Sheet ▸ A line used to control the sails. "Sheet it in," a common expression, means to tighten the mainsheet and/or jib sheet so the boat points more to weather.

Starboard ▸ The right side of the boat. Both words contain more than four letters. See "Port" for more details.

Stays ▸ Side stays, back stays, forestays are wires or metal lines that reinforce the mast, keep it in place. Perfect things to grab for stability.

Stern ▸ Back of the boat.

Telltales ▸ Red ribbons indicating wind direction. When Rubin is serious about speed—which happens any time there is another sailboat in sight—my eyes are glued to the ones fastened on the headsail and trailing the back edge (or leech) of the mainsail.

Tack ▸ To "tack" is to change the course heading on a sailboat by turning the boat into and through the wind. A "tack" is also used as a noun, describing each leg of the zigzagging path of a sailboat—as in a port or starboard "tack."

Tiller ▸ A racer's preferred steering mechanism, as one can allegedly "feel" the boat better. I prefer a wheel. It's easier to control with my feet.

Toe rail ▸ The metal or wooden rail along the sides of the boat designed to bruise the back thighs of "railmeat" on races, or smash toes on cruises. However, it does keep one from sliding off the boat when heeling.

Trapeze ▸ A cable attached to the mast and butt-bucket that allows a sailor to hike out over the water, balancing wind and boat. Hiking out in high winds is one of the few times in life more weight is better than less.

Traveler ▸ A series of lines and pulleys used in conjunction with the main sheet to adjust the trim of the mainsail.

Winch ▸ Device used to crank in the sails. Excellent upper-body training . . . especially for Rubin. Also known to scrape and bruise shins when one is not paying attention.

Windward ▸ The direction from which the wind is blowing. For example, the windward side of the sailboat is the high side—provided there is wind.

BIBLIOGRAPHY

Albert, Denis A. *Born of the Wind: An Introduction to the Ecology of Michigan Sand Dunes*. Lansing: Michigan Natural Features Inventory, 2000.

Annin, Peter. *The Great Lakes Water Wars*. Washington: Island Press, 2006.

Dempsey, Dave. *On the Brink: The Great Lakes in the 21ˢᵗ Century*. East Lansing: Michigan State University Press, 2004.

Dennis, Jerry. *The Living Great Lakes: Searching for the Heart of the Inland Seas*. New York: St. Martin's Press, 2003.

DuFresne, Jim. *The Complete Guide to Michigan Sand Dunes*. Ann Arbor: The University of Michigan Press, 2008.

Grady, Wayne. *The Great Lakes: The Natural History of a Changing Region*. Vancouver: Greystone Books, Douglas & McIntyre Publishing Group, 2007.

Husick, Charles B. *Chapman: Piloting and Seamanship*. New York: Hearst Books, 2009.

Spring, Barbara. *The Dynamic Great Lakes*. Baltimore: Independence Books, 2011.

NOTES

RELATIONSHIPS: 1978–2003

UNDER THE STARS

1. Public slips are now available at the former ferry dock and may be reserved through the Michigan Department of Natural Resources.

OPEN TO CHANGE: 2008–2012

WHISPERS OF WILDFLOWERS

2. Bridges, William. *The Way of Transition: Embracing Life's Most Difficult Moments*. New York: Perseus Publishing, 2001.

3. McKSchmidt, Mary. *Tiny Treasures: Discoveries Made Along the Lake Michigan Coast*. Livonia: Digital Books, 2011.

WHY I NO LONGER RACE

4. Two people would die that July night in 2011, as a 35-foot sailboat overturned in the storm's 65-knot winds. Both were wearing safety harnesses, securing them to the boat. It was the first accidental death in the Chicago to Mackinac race's 103-year history.

5. Husick, Charles B. *Chapman: Piloting and Seamanship*. New York: Hearst Books, 2009.

DESTINATION PORTS

6. Great Lakes Commission des Grands Lacs, "Rec boating wields a hefty economic clout in the Great Lakes," July 11, 2007. Search title at https://www.glc.org

SEARCHING FOR THE SWEET SPOT

7. Albert, Denis A. *Born of the Wind: An Introduction to the Ecology of Michigan Sand Dunes*. Lansing: Natural Features Inventory, 2000.

PROTECTING OUR HOME: 2012–2016

"WHAT IS YOUR DEEPEST DREAM?"

8. Moffatt, BettyClare. *Soulwork: Clearing the Mind, Opening the Heart, and Replenishing the Spirit*. Berkeley: Wildcat Canyon Press, 1994.

Notes

EMERGING FROM THE COCOON

9. Thanks to the people in the audience who joined me in making contributions to the Gillete Nature Association at P.J. Hoffmaster State Park, the auditorium now boasts a state-of-the-art projector that facilitates the many gifted storytellers working for, and on behalf of, the interpretive program at the park.

SEPTEMBER 2013 BLOG: TERROR IN THE STRAITS

10. Alexander, Jeff, Wallace, Beth, "Sunken Hazard," as posted by the National Wildlife Federation, October 2012. Search title at https://www.nwf.org

11. In June of 2016, President Obama signed into law the "Protecting Our Infrastructure of Pipelines and Enhancing Safety Acts of 2016." The bill is designed to enforce existing law and increases transparency and accountability, including increasing inspections of Line 5, the pipeline that runs under the Straits of Mackinac. In addition, on June 16, 2016, Enbridge announced it would be investing $7 million to buy new cleanup equipment in case there is a spill along its Line 5 pipeline.

JULY 2014 BLOG: COLD KNOWS NO PRICE

12. This was one of my most popular posts to date—a reminder of the importance of humor!

JUNE 2015 BLOG: VOICE OF A FISHERMAN'S DAUGHTER

13. I played Augusta National Golf Club in 2001, as a guest of Vern Loucks, retired Chairman and CEO of Baxter Healthcare.

Founded in 1932, Augusta National did not allow women members until eleven years later, when former Secretary of State Condoleeza Rice and South Carolina financier Darla Moore were admitted as members. Prior to that, women were allowed only as guests, minimizing the chances there would be three women in a foursome.

14. Resources:

Holey, Mark. "Lake Michigan Lake Trout Management and Restoration. www.dnr.wi.gov/topic/fishing/documents/lakemichigan/LakeTroutManagementUSFWS.pdf

Rosan, Alex, Grover, Erin, Spencer, Colby with Anderson, Patrick. "The Costs of Aquatic Invasive Species to Great Lakes States." Anderson Economic Group, LLC. 2012.

Sherburne, Morgan. "Lake Herring on Verge of Great Lakes Comeback?" October 18, 2013. www.petoskeynews.com/gaylord/sports/outdoors/wild/lake-herring-on-verge-of-great-lakes-comeback/article_baa61138-381f-11e3-8e86-001a4bcf6878.html

U.S. Geological Survey. Great Lakes Science Center. www.glsc.usgs.gov/population-restoration

NOVEMBER 2015 BLOG: THE SEARCH FOR BALANCE ON THE INDIANA SHORE

15. A copy of the 1987 Water Quality Agreement may be found at: www.ijc.org

16. Information based on the American Public Television documentary *Shifting Sands: On the Path to Sustainability* and on

presentations made by Lee Botts and the film's producer, Pat Wisniewski, of For Goodness Sake Productions, at the 2015 Healing Our Waters conference.

DECEMBER 2015 BLOG: THE ASIAN CARP CONUNDRUM

17. National Park Service. Mississippi. "Asian Carp Overview." Search article title at www.nps.gov/search/
18. Hamilton, David. The Nature Conservancy.
19. A special thanks to David Hamilton of The Nature Conservancy and David Ullrich of the Great Lakes and St. Lawrence Cities Initiative for taking the time and energy to update me on the Asian Carp conundrum. While there is a plethora of information out there on the Asian Carp, my favorites include:
Asian Carp Regional Coordinating Committee. www.asiancarp.us/index.htm
Dan Egan of the *Milwaukee Journal Sentinel* became a Pulitzer Prize finalist for his reporting on Great Lakes issues, including the Asian carp. To read his work, click on: www.jsonline.com/news/wisconsin/greatlakes-268550802.html
Michigan Senator Debbie Stabenow (D) and former Michigan Congresswoman Candice Miller (R) have taken leadership roles to ensure federal funding is available. For updates, visit www.stabenow.senate.gov
"Restoring the Natural Divide." The study was commissioned by the Great Lakes Commission and the Great Lakes and St. Lawrence Cities Initiative. Released in 2012. See: https://caws.glc.org/

"The Great Lakes and Mississippi River Interbasin Study" lists options and controls that could be used to prevent aquatic invasive species from being transferred between basins. See: http://glmris.anl.gov

JANUARY 2016 BLOG: THE SHAME OF FLINT

20. In 2014, a state-appointed emergency manager switched the source of Flint's drinking water from the Detroit municipal water sourced from Lake Huron to the corrosive Flint River. The river water was not properly treated to prevent corrosion in the aging pipes, causing lead from the pipes to leach into the drinking water, significantly elevating levels of lead in Flint residents. Research has shown there is no safe level of lead exposure.

▸ For an extensive review of the crisis, visit https://fivethirtyeight .com/features/what-went-wrong-in-flint-water-crisis-michigan/

▸ To read Michael Moore's letter to America, visit www .michaelmoore.com/DontSendBottledWater/

▸ Environmental cost of plastic water bottles, visit www .kids.nationalgeographic.com/kids/stories/spacescience/ water-bottle-pollution/

▸ For an overview on the history behind the emergency management law, https://ballotpedia.org/Michigan_ Emergency_Manager_Referendum,_Proposal_1_(2012) or www.theatlantic.com/politics/archive/2013/05/does- michigans-emergency-manager-law-disenfranchise-black- citizens/275639/

▸ For discussion on public-trust doctrine and its applicability to our water, visit www.flowforwater.org

FEBRUARY 2016 BLOG: THE WATER WARS HAVE BEGUN

21. In June of 2016, the Governors voted to approve the Waukesha diversion but with no more than an average 8.2 million gallons per day, rather than the requested 10.1 million gallons. The water is to be used to service a smaller area than originally proposed.

Resources:

Behm, Don. "Great Lakes Organization Starts Review of Waukesha's request." *Milwaukee Journal Sentinel.*

Compact Implementation Council. "Protect Our Great Lakes, Respect the Compact." www.protectourgreatlakes.org

Davey, Monica. "Waukesha Plan for Lake Michigan Water Raises Worries." *The New York Times.* August 25, 2015.

Email and/or phone conversations with Jill Crawford, Chairman of the Great Lakes Committee, Izaak Walton League of America; David Ullrich, Executive Director, Great Lakes and St. Lawrence Cities Initiative; Dave Hamilton, Senior Policy Director, Great Lakes Projects, The Nature Conservancy; Molly Flanagan, Vice President, Policy, Alliance for the Great Lakes.

LaFond, Kaye. "Waukesha Presses First Test of Great Lakes Water." *Circle of Blue.* July 9, 2014. www.circleofblue.org/2014/world/waukesha-presses-first-test-great-lakes-water-compact/

Waukesha Diversion application: www.glslregionalbody.org

Wisconsin Department of Natural Resources.

City of Waukesha Diversion Application:
https://dnr.wi.gov/topic/EIA/waukeshadiversionapp.html

APRIL 2016 BLOG: SAFELY SLATHERING SUNSCREEN

22. Resources:

5Gyres: an organization fighting ocean plastic pollution through education, science, and activism. Click on Microbeads. http://www.5gyres.org/microbeads/

Beat the Microbead, a website initiated by the Plastic Soup Foundation. Click on BeattheMicrobead. www.beatthemicrobead.org

Breast Cancer Fund: an organization working to prevent breast cancer by eliminating the exposure to toxic chemicals and radiation linked to the disease. www.bcpp.org

Great Lakes and St. Lawrence Cities Initiative, a bi-national coalition of U.S. and Canadian mayors and local officials working to advance the protection and restoration of the Great Lakes and St. Lawrence River. www.glslcities.org/initiatives/microplastics/

WINDS OF HOPE

23. Resources:

The Healing Our Waters website: www.healthylakes.org

The Great Lakes Restoration Initiative: https://www.glri.us

SEEKING BALANCE

WHY IS DIALOGUE SO DIFFICULT?

24. Resources:

Center for Nonviolent Communication. https://www.cnvc.org

Gottlieb, Lisa, MSW, SSW, nonviolent communication certified trainer. https://www.lisagottlieb.com

Rosenberg, Marshall B., PhD. *Nonviolent Communication: A Language of Life. 2nd Edition*. Encinitas: PuddleDancer Press, 2003.

ABOUT THE AUTHOR

*F*ormerly an executive for Baxter Healthcare, a Fortune 500 company, the author reinvents herself as a writer, photographer, and public speaker and journeys into uncharted waters to help build the political will necessary to clean up and protect the Great Lakes. Writing under the pen name "Mary McKSchmidt," she is a repeat contributor to *Michigan Blue* and *Sail* magazines, was a paid columnist for *The Holland Sentinel,* and has written op-ed pieces for *MLive.* Her essay "Can One Person Make a Difference?" was read in the opening session of the 2006 Great Lakes Restoration Conference, sponsored by the Healing Our Waters Coalition, more than 145 organizations advocating for the restoration and protection of the Great Lakes. Her essay "Behind the Lens of a Camera" was selected to appear in the 2016 *Bear River Review.* She is the poet and photographer of *Tiny Treasures: Discoveries Made Along the Lake Michigan Coast.* The book showcases the wildflowers found as she hiked, biked, and camped alone up the eastern coast of Lake Michigan. A natural storyteller, she has shared her adventures with audiences at garden clubs, professional women's organizations, state and county nature centers, assisted-living facilities, and environmental organizations throughout Western Michigan. Her monthly blog and "Skosh of Poetry" may be found at https://www.marymckschmidt.com or at https://www.facebook.com/mary.mckschmidt.

She and her husband, Rubin, have sailed three of the five Great Lakes, the North Channel into Georgian Bay, inland lakes throughout the Midwest, the San Juan Islands and islands in the Caribbean. And while he is not too keen on tramping through the wilderness, Rubin has accompanied her on hikes in Ireland, New Zealand, and a handful of national parks throughout the United States, and on a bicycling tour of the Netherlands.

CPSIA information can be obtained
at www.ICGtesting.com
Printed in the USA
LVHW04s1419151018
593653LV00001B/252/P